BAC 1RE/TIE

EXERCISE BOOK

Séraphine Lansonneur
Agrégée
Professeure et formatrice (75)

Anne Wilkinson
Agrégée
Professeure (49)

avec

Vincent Burgatt
Certifié
Professeur (75)

bordas
éditeur

Sommaire

VOCABULARY

🔴 Maîtriser le lexique lié aux 8 axes pour bien s'exprimer BAC

GRAMMAR

🟠 Maîtriser les 17 points de grammaire indispensables

STRATEGY

🔴 Acquérir les stratégies gagnantes pour le 🅱🅰🅲

EXAM PREP

🟢 S'entraîner efficacement au 🅱🅰🅲 grâce à la banque de sujets

Se familiariser avec les évaluations communes

BO n° 7 du 31/07/2020

Les PDF des nouvelles évaluations du *accompagnées de leurs grilles d'évaluation sont sur le site lycee.editions-bordas.fr.*

En classe de 1re

Évaluation 1 ▶ 2e trimestre – 20 points – 20 minutes

Niveaux visés : LVA = **B1** – LVB = **A2-B1**

Compréhension de l'oral
– Communication du titre du document support de l'évaluation et éventuellement des noms propres – Document audio ou vidéo d'1 min 30 maximum – 3 écoutes espacées d'1 min (prise de notes possible lors de l'écoute) – Compte-rendu du document en français de manière libre ou guidée

Évaluation 2 ▶ 3e trimestre – 20 points – 1 heure 30

Niveaux visés : LVA = **B1-B2** – LVB = **A2-B1**
Le sujet est remis en intégralité au début. Le candidat organise son temps comme il l'entend.

Compréhension de l'écrit 10 points	Expression écrite 10 points
– 1 ou 2 textes – Longueur cumulée des textes = entre 2 300 et 4 000 signes – Compte-rendu en français ou en en anglais selon la consigne du ou des texte(s) de manière libre ou guidée	– 1 ou 2 questions en lien avec la thématique générale du ou des supports de la compréhension de l'écrit – Document iconographique possible – Rédaction en anglais

En classe de Tle

Évaluation 3 ▶ 3e trimestre – 20 points
(10 points pour la compréhension • 10 points pour l'expression)

PARTIE 1 : écrit – étude de dossier

Niveaux visés : LVA = **B2** – LVB = **B1**
Durée : 1 heure 30. Le sujet est remis en intégralité au début. Le candidat organise son temps comme il l'entend.

Compréhension de l'oral	Compréhension de l'écrit	Expression écrite
– Communication du titre du document support de l'évaluation et éventuellement des noms propres – Document audio ou vidéo d'1 min 30 maximum – 3 écoutes espacées d'1 min (prise de notes possible lors de l'écoute) – Compte-rendu du document en français de manière libre ou guidée	– 1 ou 2 textes – Longueur cumulée des textes = entre 2 500 et 4 300 signes – Compte-rendu en français ou en anglais selon la consigne du ou des textes – Il peut en outre être demandé de répondre en français ou en anglais à une question portant sur la compréhension de l'ensemble du dossier	– 1 ou 2 questions en lien avec la thématique générale du dossier – Document iconographique possible – Rédaction en anglais

PARTIE 2 : oral

Durée : 10 min + 10 min de préparation – Choix entre 3 axes. Niveaux visés : LVA = **B2** – LVB = **B1**

Expression orale en continu	Expression orale en interaction
– Expression à partir d'un document, au choix parmi 2 documents iconographiques ou 2 citations ou 1 document iconographique et 1 citation – 5 min pour justifier quel document ou quelle illustration illustre le mieux l'axe choisi et pourquoi	Échange avec l'examinateur sur des questions plus générales portant, par exemple, sur le travail réalisé en classe sur l'axe choisi

Réussir les évaluations grâce à des stratégies gagnantes et un entraînement régulier

Votre *exercise book* est composé de quatre parties : **Vocabulary**, **Grammar**, **Strategy** et **Exam Prep**.

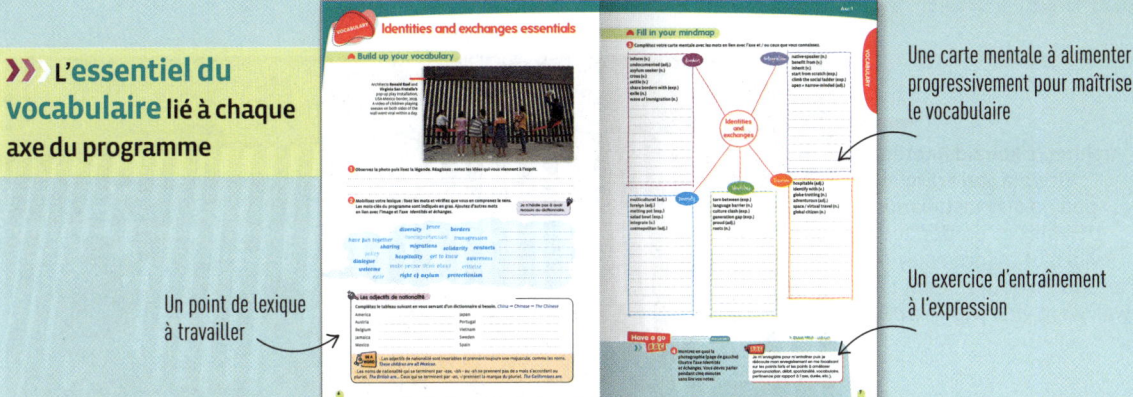

»» L'**essentiel du vocabulaire** lié à chaque axe du programme

Une carte mentale à alimenter progressivement pour maîtriser le vocabulaire

Un exercice d'entraînement à l'expression

Un point de lexique à travailler

»» Les **points de grammaire** indispensables

La règle

Les exercices d'application

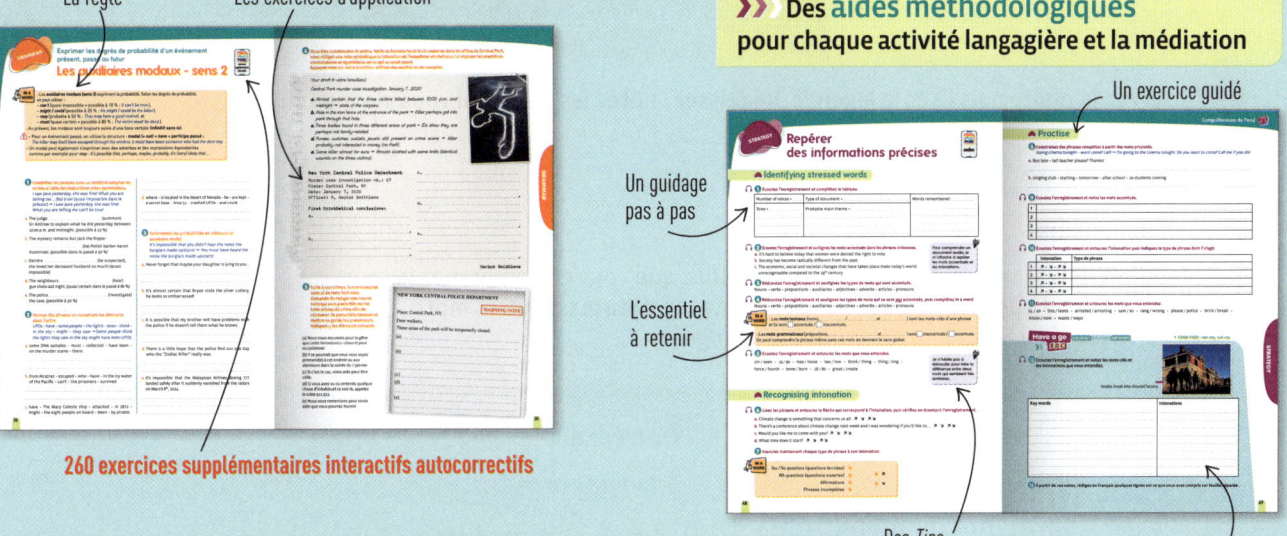

260 exercices supplémentaires interactifs autocorrectifs

»» Des **aides méthodologiques** pour chaque activité langagière et la médiation

Un exercice guidé

Un guidage pas à pas

L'essentiel à retenir

Des *Tips*

Un exercice d'application à faire en autonomie

»» Un **entraînement** en autonomie aux **3 évaluations du BAC**

Ici, un exemple de l'évaluation 3

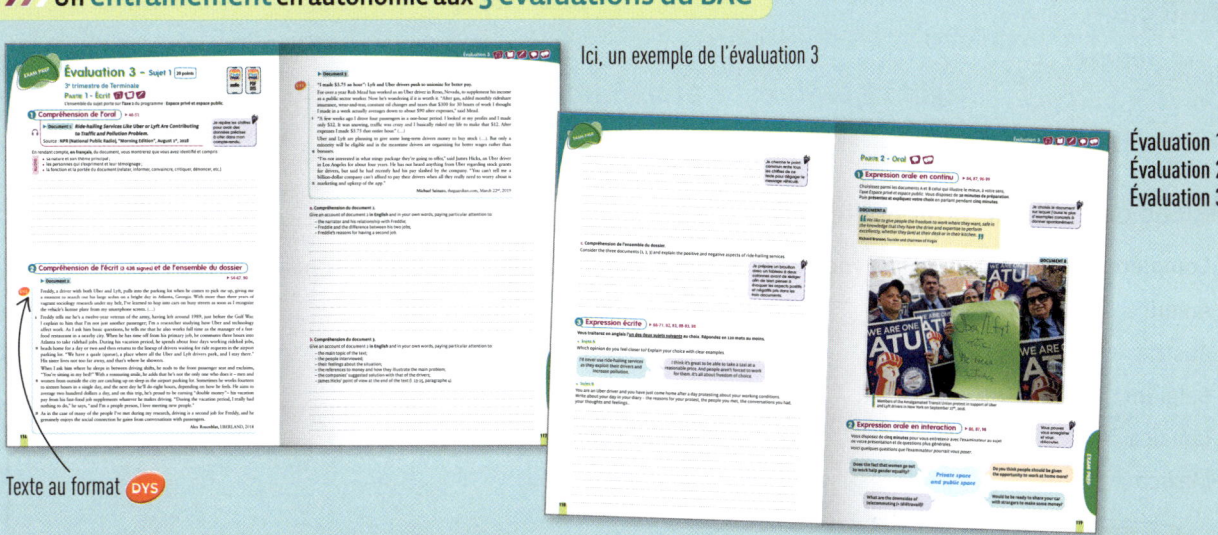

Texte au format DYS

Évaluation 1 : 4 sujets
Évaluation 2 : 3 sujets
Évaluation 3 : 3 sujets

🎧 compréhension de l'oral (audio ou vidéo) – 📖 compréhension de l'écrit
💬 expression orale en continu – 🗨 expression orale en interaction – ✏ expression écrite

ressources accessibles via Bordas Flash Page  ou sur le site lycee.editions-bordas.fr

Identities and exchanges essentials

🔺 Build up your vocabulary

Architects **Ronald Rael** and **Virginia San Fratello's** pop-up play installation, USA-Mexico border, 2019. A video of children playing seesaw on both sides of the wall went viral within a day.

1 Observez la photo puis lisez la légende. Réagissez : notez les idées qui vous viennent à l'esprit.

....

....

2 Mobilisez votre lexique : lisez les mots et vérifiez que vous en comprenez le sens. Les mots-clés du programme sont indiqués en gras. Ajoutez d'autres mots en lien avec l'image et l'axe *Identités et échanges*.

> Je n'hésite pas à avoir recours au dictionnaire.

diversity fence **borders**
have fun together incomprehension transgression
sharing **migrations** **solidarity** **contacts**
policy **hospitality** get to know awareness
dialogue make people think about criticise
welcome
exile **right of asylum** **protectionism**

🔍 Les adjectifs de nationalité

Complétez le tableau suivant en vous servant d'un dictionnaire si besoin. *China → Chinese → The Chinese*

America	....	Japan	....
Austria	....	Portugal	....
Belgium	....	Vietnam	....
Jamaica	....	Sweden	....
Mexico	....	Spain	....

 **IN A WORD**

• Les adjectifs de nationalité sont invariables et prennent toujours une majuscule, comme les noms. *These children are all Mexican.*

• Les noms de nationalité qui se terminent par *-ese*, *-ish* - ou *-sh* ne prennent pas de s mais s'accordent au pluriel. *The British are...* Ceux qui se terminent par *-an*, *-i* prennent la marque du pluriel. *The Californians are.*

🔺 Fill in your mindmap

3 Complétez votre carte mentale avec les mots en lien avec l'axe et / ou ceux que vous connaissez.

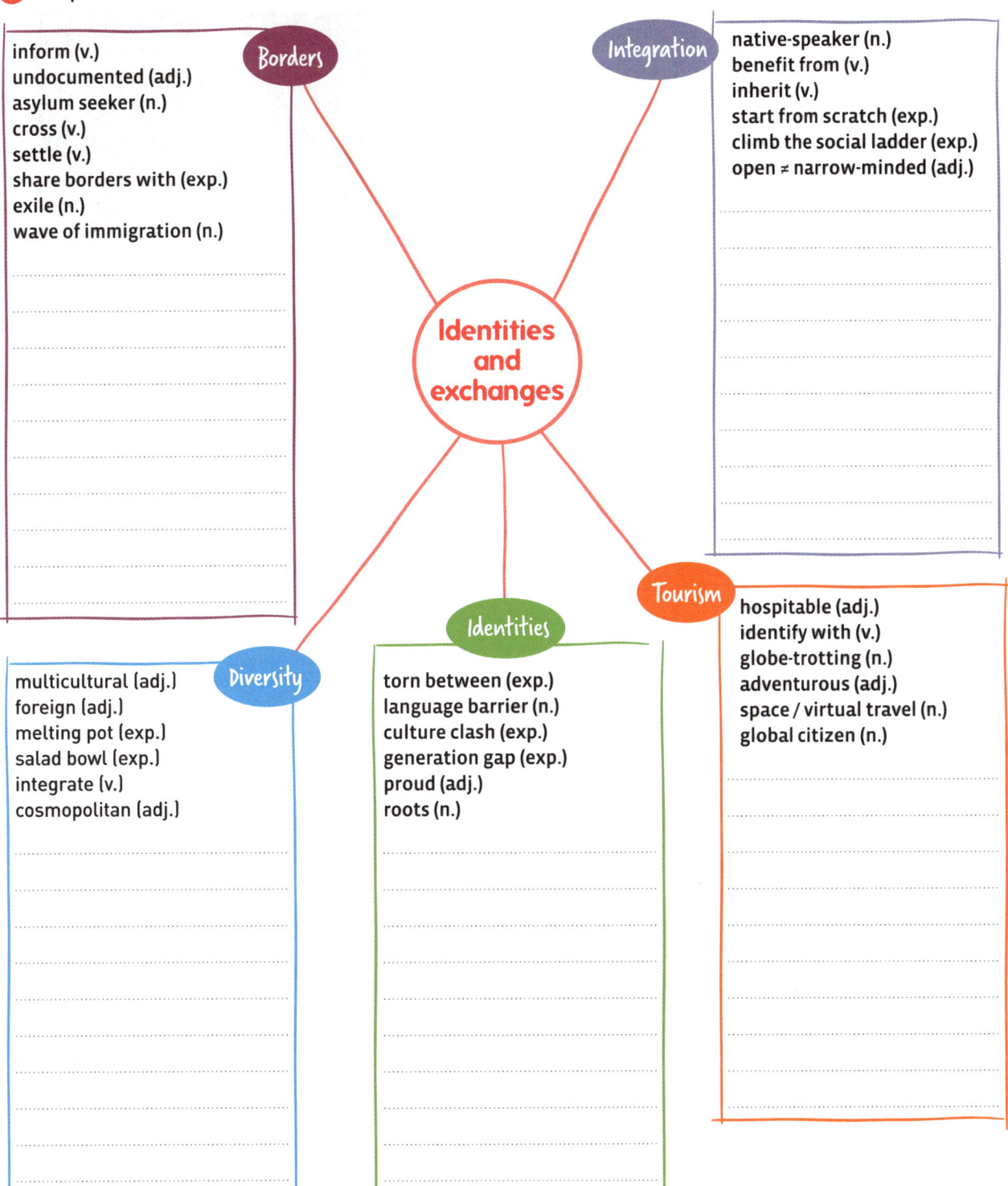

Borders
- inform (v.)
- undocumented (adj.)
- asylum seeker (n.)
- cross (v.)
- settle (v.)
- share borders with (exp.)
- exile (n.)
- wave of immigration (n.)

Integration
- native-speaker (n.)
- benefit from (v.)
- inherit (v.)
- start from scratch (exp.)
- climb the social ladder (exp.)
- open ≠ narrow-minded (adj.)

Identities and exchanges

Diversity
- multicultural (adj.)
- foreign (adj.)
- melting pot (exp.)
- salad bowl (exp.)
- integrate (v.)
- cosmopolitan (adj.)

Identities
- torn between (exp.)
- language barrier (n.)
- culture clash (exp.)
- generation gap (exp.)
- proud (adj.)
- roots (n.)

Tourism
- hospitable (adj.)
- identify with (v.)
- globe-trotting (n.)
- adventurous (adj.)
- space / virtual travel (n.)
- global citizen (n.)

Have a go BAC ÉVALUATION 1 ÉVALUATION 2 **ÉVALUATION 3**

➤ **EXAM PREP • 116-127**

4 Montrez en quoi la photographie (page de gauche) illustre l'axe *Identités et échanges*. Vous devez parler pendant cinq minutes sans lire vos notes.

BAC Je m'enregistre pour m'entraîner puis je réécoute mon enregistrement en me focalisant sur les points forts et les points à améliorer (prononciation, débit, spontanéité, vocabulaire, pertinence par rapport à l'axe, durée, etc.).

Private space and public space essentials

Build up your vocabulary

" *When at 15, my girlfriends started dropping out of their beloved sports teams, because they didn't want to appear muscly, when at 18, my male friends were unable to express their feelings, I decided that I was a feminist.* "

Emma Watson, British actor and Goodwill Ambassador for U.N. Women, September 20th, 2014

1 Lisez la légende et la citation. Réagissez : notez les idées qui vous viennent à l'esprit.

....

....

2 Mobilisez votre lexique : lisez les mots et vérifiez que vous en comprenez le sens. Les mots-clés du programme sont indiqués en gras. Ajoutez d'autres mots en lien avec la citation et l'axe *Espace privé et espace public*.

> Je n'hésite pas à avoir recours au dictionnaire.

intolerance   **gender equality**

peer group pressure   acceptance   make fun of

stereotypes   **parity**

blurred lines   **education**   ashamed   awkward

feminism

   be oneself

prejudiced   discriminate against

male chauvinism   **emancipation**

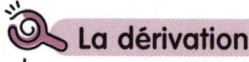 **La dérivation**

Ajoutez des préfixes ou des suffixes pour créer autant de nouveaux mots que possible à partir des mots racines. Indiquez la catégorie grammaticale des mots obtenus.
fair (adj.) ➡ *unfair (adj.) – fairness (n.) – fairly (adv.)*

préfixe	suffixe
-un	-ful
-in	-dom
-dis	-ity
-im	-ment
-in	-ly
	-ic
	-al
	-ist
	-ism
	-ise

a. law (n.): ....

b. wise (adj.): ....

c. place (v./n.): ....

....

d. possible (adj.): ....

e. feminine (adj.): ....

f. able (ajd.): ....

> **IN A WORD**
>
> • La dérivation permet de modifier le sens d'un mot grâce à un préfixe ou un suffixe placé avant ou après le mot racine. *fair ➡ unfair*.
>
> • La catégorie grammaticale peut alors changer. *economic (adj.) ➡ economically (adv.)*.
>
> Comme en français, plusieurs préfixes / suffixes peuvent s'enchaîner. *economy + -ic + -al + -ly = economically*

VOCABULARY

🔴 Fill in your mindmap

3 Complétez votre carte mentale avec les mots en lien avec l'axe et / ou ceux que vous connaissez.

Gender equality

gender roles (n.)
equal pay (n.)
glass ceiling (exp.)
achievement (n.)
household chores (n.)
stay-at-home (adj.)

Places

outdoors ≠ indoors (n.)
get-together (n.)
prohibited (adj.)
socialise (v.)
hang out (v.)
home town (n.)

Private space and public space

The working world

commute (v.)
teleworking (n.)
flexible working hours (exp.)
full-time ≠ part-time (adj.)
self-sufficient (adj.)
successful (adj.)

Family life

cohabitation (n.)
move forward (v.)
nuclear family (n.)
blended family (exp.)
single-parent (exp.)
same-sex marriage (exp.)

Changes

blurred (adj.)
threshold (n.)
go through (v.)
limitless (adj.)
similar (to) (adj.)
evolve (v.)

Have a go BAC

ÉVALUATION 1   ÉVALUATION 2   **ÉVALUATION 3**

➤ **EXAM PREP • 116-127**

4 Montrez en quoi la citation (page de gauche) illustre l'axe *Espace privé et espace public.* Vous devez parler pendant cinq minutes sans lire vos notes.

🔴 BAC

Je m'enregistre pour m'entraîner puis je réécoute mon enregistrement en me focalisant sur les points forts et les points à améliorer (prononciation, débit, spontanéité, vocabulaire, pertinence par rapport à l'axe, durée, etc.).

Art and power essentials

🔺 Build up your vocabulary

Mural by Hawaiian artist **Hula** (Sean Yoro), Bay of Fundy, Canada, 2017 – *"I hope [the murals] ignite a sense of urgency, as they represent the millions of people in need of our help who are already being affected from the rising sea levels of climate change."*

1 Observez la photo puis lisez la légende et la citation. Réagissez : notez les idées qui vous viennent à l'esprit.

....

....

....

2 Mobilisez votre lexique : lisez les mots et vérifiez que vous en comprenez le sens. Les mots-clés du programme sont indiqués en gras. Ajoutez d'autres mots en lien avec l'image et l'axe *Art et pouvoir*.

> 💡 Je n'hésite pas à avoir recours au dictionnaire.

tornado *defy* ***resistance***
challenge authority *climate change* *larger-than-life*
defend *storm*
rising water levels *inform* *mural*
promote *manmade catastrophe* *cyclone*
committed art
protest art *environmental disaster* *torrential rain*
melt *greenhouse gas* *out of one's depth*

....
....
....
....
....
....

Les adjectifs en *-ed* ou *-ing*

Ajoutez *-ed* ou *-ing* à la base verbale pour former un adjectif.
The painting was so shocking that the gallery refused to exhibit it.

a. The artist wanted to show that people were still being discriminat............ against.

b. I find his graffiti both annoy............ and interest............ .

c. It's frighten............ to think that some protest artists are oppress............ .

d. Art used for propaganda is really irritat............ .

e. I'm surpris............ that any artist would accept to produce a work of art for propaganda.

IN A WORD

• Un adjectif en *-ed* décrit une émotion ou un état.
I was confused.

• Un adjectif en *-ing* décrit la cause d'une émotion ou d'un état.
The film was boring.

🏴 En général, les adjectifs en *-ed* se traduisent, en français, par un adjectif en *-é(e)* (*fatigué(e)*) et les adjectifs en *-ing* par un adjectif en *-ant(e)* (*fatigant(e)*).

🔺 Fill in your mindmap

3 Complétez votre carte mentale avec les mots en lien avec l'axe et / ou ceux que connaissez.

Aim

inform (v.)
serve a cause (exp.)
support (v.)
defend (v.)
promote (v.)
embellish (v.)

Official art

propaganda (n.)
censorship (n.)
brainwash (v.)
patriotic films (n.)
institutional building (n.)
official portrait (n.)

Art and power

Empowerment

challenge (n., v.)
seek recognition (exp.)
committed (adj.)
defy (v.)
rebellious (adj.)
influential (adj.)

Counter-culture

underground (n.)
resistance (n.)
satire (n.)
street art (n.)
protest art (n.)
challenge authority (exp.)

Forms of art

architecture (n.)
literature (n.)
painting (n.)
cinema (n.)
caricatures (n.)
music (n.)
cartoon (n.)

Have a go BAC

ÉVALUATION 1 ÉVALUATION 2 **ÉVALUATION 3**

➤ **EXAM PREP • 116-127**

4 Montrez en quoi la photographie (page de gauche) illustre l'axe *Art et pouvoir*. Vous devez parler pendant cinq minutes sans lire vos notes.

 BAC

Je m'enregistre pour m'entraîner puis je réécoute mon enregistrement en me focalisant sur les points forts et les points à améliorer (prononciation, débit, spontanéité, vocabulaire, pertinence par rapport à l'axe, durée, etc.).

Citizenship and virtual worlds essentials

🔺 Build up your vocabulary

Fake news is false information that is often spread using social media.

> ❝*Everyone is entitled to his own opinion, but not to his own facts.*❞
>
> **Daniel Patrick Moynihan** (1927-2003) served as an ambassador, a senator, and an adviser to four US presidents.

1 Lisez la citation. Réagissez : notez les idées qui vous viennent à l'esprit.

....

....

....

2 Mobilisez votre lexique : lisez les mots et vérifiez que vous en comprenez le sens. Les mots-clés du programme sont indiqués en gras. Ajoutez d'autres mots en lien avec la citation et l'axe *Citoyenneté et mondes virtuels*.

💡 Je n'hésite pas à avoir recours au dictionnaire.

> truth   persuade   propaganda
> **censorship and Internet control** form an opinion
> tell a lie **freedom of expression** deceive journalist
> discredit / debunk suspicious **media education**
> politician **forums** official news sources bias
> misinformation **fake news** blogs **manipulation**
> **social networks** amateur

....
....
....
....
....

🔍 Do et make

Complétez les phrases avec *do* ou *make*. Vérifiez dans un dictionnaire.
They will (...) all they can to publish the truth.
→ *They will do all they can to publish the truth.*

a. Good journalists .... their best to be objective.

b. It takes time but I always .... an effort to check my sources of information.

c. I'd like to .... a suggestion to improve the quality of our online magazine.

d. Spreading lies about people can really .... a lot of damage.

e. I don't usually share fake news but everyone can .... a mistake.

IN A WORD 🏴󠁧󠁢󠁥󠁮󠁧󠁿 *Do* et *make* signifient tous les deux « faire » en français.

● *Do* signifie « faire » en français dans le sens d'accomplir une activité. ***What are you doing?***

● Le plus souvent, *make* exprime l'idée de fabriquer, de produire, avec un résultat concret. ***They made a list.***

● Il y a des expressions toutes faites qu'il faut apprendre par cœur : *make a living, do harm*.

🔺 Fill in your mindmap

3 Complétez votre carte mentale avec les mots en lien avec l'axe et / ou ceux que vous connaissez.

Social media

social network (n.)
virtual community (exp.)
blog (n.)
forum (n.)
share (v.)
follower (n.)

Information

education (n.)
censorship (n.)
wikis (n.)
e-zine (n.)
browse (v.)
search (v.)

Citizenship and virtual worlds

Expression

freedom of expression (n.)
censorship (n.)
reach a wide audience (exp.)
speak one's mind (exp.)
outspoken (adj.)
anonymous (adj.)

Risks

identity theft (n.)
cyberbullying (n.)
manipulate (v.)
personal data (n.)
virtual payment (n.)
isolate (v.)

Responsibility

Internet control (n.)
participatory democracy (n.)
whistleblower (n.)
aware (adj.)
media literacy (n.)
distinguish (v.)

ÉVALUATION 1 ÉVALUATION 2 **ÉVALUATION 3**

➤ **EXAM PREP • 116-127**

4 Montrez en quoi la citation (page de gauche) illustre l'axe *Citoyenneté et mondes virtuels*. Vous devez parler pendant cinq minutes sans lire vos notes.

 **BAC**

Je m'enregistre pour m'entraîner puis je réécoute mon enregistrement en me focalisant sur les points forts et les points à améliorer (prononciation, débit, spontanéité, vocabulaire, pertinence par rapport à l'axe, durée, etc.).

Fictions and realities essentials

🔴 Build up your vocabulary

❝ It's not speculation, it's true! Mobile phones, laptops, tablets, the Internet, all were predicted and dreamed up in science fiction first. (...) I don't just make random things up. I consider the world around me. I live in it. I experience it. I love it. I hate it. I worry about it. Then I imagine what's to come. ❞

Nnedi Okorafor, "Exclusive Interview with Nigerian Science Fiction Writer, Nnedi Okorafor", *Ventures Africa*, September 23rd, 2015

2001: A Space Odyssey, **Stanley Kubrick**, 1968. The suitcase in this 1968 film contains all the components of a modern laptop computer such as a keyboard, a camera, a digital file storage and a display screen.

1 Lisez la citation. Réagissez : notez les idées qui vous viennent à l'esprit.

....
....
....
....

2 Mobilisez votre lexique : lisez les mots et vérifiez que vous en comprenez le sens. Les mots-clés du programme sont indiqués en gras. Ajoutez d'autres mots en lien avec le sujet évoqué dans la citation et l'axe *Fictions et réalités*.

💡 Je n'hésite pas à avoir recours au dictionnaire.

leading lights technology **utopias**
dystopias device predict foreshadow
stereotypes **legends** make sth up
prejudiced **beliefs** visionary
science fiction **(super-) heroes / heroines**
ahead of one's time

🐌 Varier les adjectifs

Classez les adjectifs ci-dessous dans le tableau en fonction de leur signification. Utilisez un dictionnaire si nécessaire.

inspirational – disappointing – amazing – poor – unconvincing – heart-breaking – unforgettable – awesome – convincing – emotional – comical – moving – heart-rending – brilliant – atrocious – uplifting – light-hearted – hysterical – entertaining – poignant – hilarious – dreadful – tragic

IN A WORD
● Il est important de varier les adjectifs pour nuancer et préciser sa pensée. *good → amazing.*

● Pour ne pas toujours utiliser *very* devant un adjectif, mobilisez vos connaissances et cherchez des synonymes dans un dictionnaire.

very good	very bad	very funny	very sad

🔺 Fill in your mindmap

3 Complétez votre carte mentale avec les mots en lien avec l'axe et / ou ceux que vous connaissez.

Tales

belief (n.)
legendary (adj.)
mythical (adj.)
myth (n.)
legend (n.)
cross-cultural (adj.)

Role

inspirational (adj.)
transcend (v.)
creativity (n.)
escape (v.)
get away from (v.)
warn (v.)

Fictions and realities

Real-life impact

heroic (adj.)
iconic (adj.)
embody (v.)
every-day life (exp.)
role model (n.)
empowerment (n.)

Science fiction

travel in space (exp.)
spaceship (n.)
visionary (adj.)
android (n.)
utopia ≠ dystopia (n.)
intergalactic (adj.)

Inheritance

legacy (n.)
cultural (adj.)
national feeling (n.)
respect (v.)
value (n.)
convey (v.)

 **Have a go**

EVALUATION 1 · EVALUATION 2 · **ÉVALUATION 3**

➤ **EXAM PREP · 116-127**

4 Montrez en quoi la citation (page de gauche) illustre l'axe *Fictions et réalités*. Vous devez parler pendant cinq minutes sans lire vos notes.

 **BAC**

Je m'enregistre pour m'entraîner puis je réécoute mon enregistrement en me focalisant sur les points forts et les points à améliorer (prononciation, débit, spontanéité, vocabulaire, pertinence par rapport à l'axe, durée, etc.).

Scientific innovation and responsibility essentials

🔴 Build up your vocabulary

Volunteers participate in numerous activities such as urban gardening, street cleaning, recycling waste, and converting abandoned lots in areas suffering from urban decay.

1 Observez la photo puis lisez la légende. Réagissez : notez les idées qui vous viennent à l'esprit.

....

....

....

....

2 Mobilisez votre lexique : lisez les mots et vérifiez que vous en comprenez le sens. Les mots-clés du programme sont indiqués en gras. Ajoutez d'autres mots en lien avec l'image et l'axe *Innovations scientifiques et responsabilité*.

> Je n'hésite pas à avoir recours au dictionnaire.

eco-citizen   *vacant lots*   *industrial*

local distribution network   *bottom-up project*

convert / repurpose   *plant*   *neighbourhood*

dilapidated   **organic**   **green growth**

pollution   *environmentally-friendly*

          poverty   *deprived*

....
....
....
....
....
....

🐌 Le paradoxe

Reliez les deux phrases à l'aide du mot de liaison indiqué en faisant les changements nécessaires.
He hated gardening. / He helped plant some trees. (in spite of)
→ *In spite of (his/him) hating gardening, he helped plant some trees.*

a. It's a lot of work. Everyone has a good time. (although)

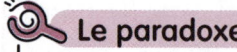

b. Some countries are hesitant about changing. We cannot give up. (despite)

....

c. This teenager has been a major inspiration. She is very young. (in spite of)

....

IN A WORD

• Certains mots permettent de relier deux actions ou situations lorsque la relation entre ces deux faits est paradoxale.
The students have little free time. They have become volunteers. → *Although the students have little free time they have become volunteers.*

• *Although / even though* sont suivis de phrases. *Despite* et *in spite of* sont suivis d'un nom ou d'un pronom.

🔺 Fill in your mindmap

3 Complétez votre carte mentale avec les mots en lien avec l'axe et / ou ceux que vous connaissez.

Scientific innovation
- robot (n.)
- nanotechnology (n.)
- space exploration (n.)
- break new boundaries (exp.)
- innovate (v.)
- state-of-the-art (exp.)

Environment
- renewable energy (n.)
- recycling (n.)
- biodiversity (n.)
- green growth (n.)
- transport (n.)
- carbon footprint (exp.)

Scientific innovation and responsibility

Issues
- GMO (n.)
- arms race (n.)
- overpopulation (n.)
- workplace alienation (n.)
- pollution (n.)
- sectarianism (n.)

Medical progress
- genetic research (n.)
- vaccine (n.)
- cloning (n.)
- save lives (exp.)
- improve life quality (exp.)
- life expectancy (n.)

Responsibility
- carpooling (n.)
- local distribution network (n.)
- organic (adj.)
- rallying (n.)
- reduce consumption (v.)
- eco-citizen (exp.)

EVALUATION 1 EVALUATION 2 **ÉVALUATION 3**

4 Montrez en quoi l'image (page de gauche) illustre l'axe *Innovations scientifiques et responsabilité*. Vous devez parler pendant cinq minutes sans lire vos notes.

> **EXAM PREP • 116-127**

🎙 **BAC**

Je m'enregistre pour m'entraîner puis je réécoute mon enregistrement en me focalisant sur les points forts et les points à améliorer (prononciation, débit, spontanéité, vocabulaire, pertinence par rapport à l'axe, durée, etc.).

Diversity and inclusion essentials

🔴 Build up your vocabulary

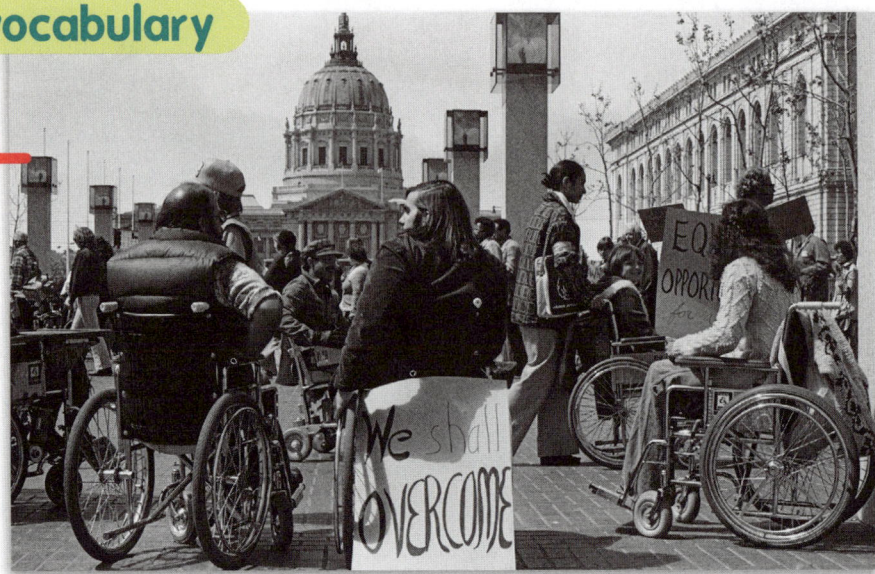

Protest for legal rights for people with disabilities, San Francisco, 1977. This sit-in was the longest ever non-violent occupation of a US federal building, and helped change the laws.

1 Observez la photo puis lisez la légende. Réagissez : notez les idées qui vous viennent à l'esprit.

....
....
....
....

2 Mobilisez votre lexique : lisez les mots et vérifiez que vous en comprenez le sens. Les mots-clés du programme sont indiqués en gras. Ajoutez d'autres mots en lien avec l'image et l'axe *Diversité et inclusion*.

> 💡 Je n'hésite pas à avoir recours au dictionnaire.

protest   wheelchair   facilities

disability   accessible   fight for one's rights

ramp   **freedom of movement**   deserve   initiative

special needs   inclusive   **discriminations**

join in   **minorities**   legal rights   court case

campaign   tribunal   demonstrate   **integration**

equality   recognition   fit in

....
....
....
....
....

🐌 Phrasal verbs

Remplacez les mots entre parenthèses avec un verbe à particule synonyme choisi dans cette liste : *bring about – let down – speak out – leave out – give up – fit in.*
The students ... (voiced their opinion) against exclusion in their school.
→ *The students spoke out against exclusion in their school.*

a. At first enthusiastic about his new school, Mike soon felt .... (disappointed).

b. He found it hard to .... (blend in) at first because of his disability .

c. The other students didn't deliberately .... (exclude him).

d. Mike has decided not to .... (abandon) hope.

e. He will talk to his classmates about his disability and this will .... (provoke) change.

>  **IN A WORD**
> • Un verbe peut être suivi de différentes particules et donc avoir différents sens :
> *let* = permettre ;
> *let in* = faire entrer.
>
> • Lorsque ces verbes sont employés avec un pronom complément, ce dernier s'intercale entre le verbe et la particule :
> *I read it through.*

🔺 Fill in your mindmap

3 Complétez votre carte mentale avec les mots en lien avec l'axe et / ou ceux que vous connaissez.

Diversity

different abilities (n.)
unrecognised languages (n.)
generational (adj.)
minorities (n.)
idiolects (n.)
enrich (v.)

Inclusion

integrated (adj.)
self-determination (n.)
special needs (n.)
accessibility (n.)
join in (v.)
freedom of movement (exp.)

Diversity and inclusion

Means of action

demonstrate (v.)
petition (n.)
debate (v.)
live together (v.)
vote (v.)
campaign (n., v.)

Challenges

discrimination (n.)
ignorance (n.)
narrow-minded (adj.)
health issue (n.)
prejudice (n.)
stereotype (n.)

Society

changing norms (n.)
evolve (v.)
individual rights (n.)
social norms (n.)
laws (n.)
policy (n.)

 **Have a go BAC**

ÉVALUATION 1   ÉVALUATION 2   **ÉVALUATION 3**

➤ **EXAM PREP • 116-127**

4 Montrez en quoi la photographie (page de gauche) illustre l'axe *Diversité et inclusion*. Vous devez parler pendant cinq minutes sans lire vos notes.

 **BAC**

Je m'enregistre pour m'entraîner puis je réécoute mon enregistrement en me focalisant sur les points forts et les points à améliorer (prononciation, débit, spontanéité, vocabulaire, pertinence par rapport à l'axe, durée, etc.).

Territory and memory essentials

◢ Build up your vocabulary

1940 weekend at **The Black Country Living Museum**, Dudley, UK, 2016. The Black Country Living Museum is an open-air museum portraying 300 years of history, with a focus on 1850-1950.

1 Observez la photo puis lisez la légende. Réagissez : notez les idées qui vous viennent à l'esprit.

....

....

....

2 Mobilisez votre lexique : lisez les mots et vérifiez que vous en comprenez le sens. Les mots-clés du programme sont indiqués en gras. Ajoutez d'autres mots en lien avec l'image et l'axe *Territoire et mémoire*.

> Je n'hésite pas à avoir recours au dictionnaire.

miner   dress up   **official history**   coal

built heritage   interactive   take part in   factory

back-to-backs   terraced houses   commemorate

working-class   industrial city   turn back the clock

traces of history   preserve the past   **historic district**

remember how things were   heavy industry

....

....

....

....

....

Les faux amis

Lisez le texte. Associez les mots soulignés à leur synonyme puis reliez-les à leur traduction.

The Black Museum looks like an <u>inhabited</u> village whereas it's <u>actually</u> an interactive museum with actors. Going there gives you a <u>comprehensive</u> idea of life during the industrial revolution and the <u>habits</u> of people at that time. It's really an amazing <u>achievement</u> to have created it. I <u>attended</u> the opening and I was impressed.

		Synonyme	Traduction
1	inhabited	● ● custom	● ● accomplissement
2	actually	● ● accomplishment	● ● habité
3	comprehensive	● ● be present at	● ● habitude
4	habit	● ● lived in	● ● en fait
5	achievement	● ● complete	● ● assister à
6	attend	● ● in fact	● ● complet

IN A WORD 🔵 On appelle « faux amis » les mots qui se ressemblent d'une langue à l'autre mais dont le sens diffère. Il faut se servir du contexte pour éviter des erreurs d'interprétation.
I resumed my visit of the museum. = J'ai continué ma visite du musée.

● Pensez à lister et apprendre par cœur les faux amis rencontrés lors de vos lectures.

🔴 Fill in your mindmap

3 Complétez votre carte mentale avec les mots en lien avec l'axe et / ou ceux que vous connaissez.

Places and traces

museum (n.)
battlefield (n.)
historic district (n.)
built heritage (n.)
border areas (n.)
war memorial (n.)

Marking eras

industrial revolution (n.)
World Wars (n.)
mass emigration (n.)
globalisation (n.)
Victorian (adj.)
the British Empire (n.)

Territory and memory

Influential people

role model (n.)
counter model (n.)
pioneer (n.)
heroic (adj.)
break the mold (exp.)
lead the way (exp.)

Memory

official history (n.)
duty of remembrance (n.)
commemorate (v.)
library (n.)
amnesia (n.)
lest we forget (exp.)

Legacy

democracy (n.)
multicultural (adj.)
women's rights (n.)
historic buildings (n.)
traumatised (adj.)
transform (v.)

 **Have a go** ÉVALUATION 1 ÉVALUATION 2 **ÉVALUATION 3**

➤ **EXAM PREP • 116-127**

4 Montrez en quoi la photographie (page de gauche) illustre l'axe *Territoire et mémoire*. Vous devez parler pendant cinq minutes sans lire vos notes.

Je m'enregistre pour m'entraîner puis je réécoute mon enregistrement en me focalisant sur les points forts et les points à améliorer (prononciation, débit, spontanéité, vocabulaire, pertinence par rapport à l'axe, durée, etc.).

GRAMMAR

Exprimer des habitudes, des opinions,
des actions en cours et futures

Le présent simple / le présent en *be + V-ing*

bordas
Flash PAGE
exercices
supplémentaires
interactifs

IN A WORD

- Le **présent simple** exprime des actions récurrentes, des vérités générales, des opinions, et sert à raconter une histoire (présent de narration). *George Orwell's story **takes place** in 1984..., the main characters **are**...*

- Le **présent simple** s'emploie avec les auxiliaires **do / does** aux formes interrogatives et négatives. ***Do** new technologies **impact** our carbon footprint? I **don't think** so.*

- Le **présent en *be + V-ing*** exprime une action en cours ou une intention future. *My friend **is using** his smartphone in class, he **is surfing** on the web. I'**m buying** the newest smartphone tomorrow.*

- Le **présent en *be + V-ing*** s'emploie avec **be** à toutes les formes. ***Be** varie selon le sujet (am / are / is).*

⚠️ 🇬🇧 – **Be + V-ing** s'emploie très rarement avec les verbes d'état (*be, belong, seem*, etc.), de goût (*love, want*, etc.), et d'opinion (*think, consider*, etc.).
– **Do** peut s'utiliser à la forme affirmative pour insister sur le verbe : *Sending e-mails **does** impact the carbon footprint!*
➜ Envoyer des e-mails a un **réel** effet sur l'empreinte carbone !

"Stop telling me to live in the present!"

1 Complétez les phrases suivantes en utilisant le présent simple ou le présent en *be + V-ing*.
Paul (now / listen) to his English teacher, he (not / send) any messages with his smartphone in class anymore!
➜ *Paul is now listening to his English teacher, he isn't sending any messages with his smartphone in class anymore!*

a. — ....(really / think) that our
parents ....(go to buy / us)
smartphones for Christmas?
— I ....(hope) so.

b. ....(not / use) my old laptop
anymore, the new one ....
(work / much better).

c. ....(you / joke)? This tablet
....(cost) so much!

d. I ....(not / think) that everyone
....(realise) how much our
planet ....(really / suffer).

e. ....(Pamela / not / realise)
she ....(be) addicted to her smartphone?

2 Construisez des phrases à partir des éléments donnés.
A: Who / Jane / talk to / ? B: her neighbour ➜ *A: Who is Jane talking to? B: Jane / She is talking to her neighbour.*

a. A: When / you / buy / that new video game / ? B: not today
A: ....
B: ....

b. A: How / I / go / to phone my friends / ?
B: with my new smartphone.
A: ....
B: ....

c. A: Why / Peter / shout at / Tom / so loudly?
B: using his video game.
A: ....
B: ....

d. A: How many laptops / sell / Richard / a day?
B: twenty laptops a day.
A: ....
....
B: ....

3 Posez les questions correspondant aux éléments manquants.
I enjoy playing (...). ➜ *What do you enjoy playing?*

a. I like posting (...) on the web.
....
....

b. I often Google (...) on the web.
....
....

c. Harry wants to become a (...) when he is older.
....
....

d. Kathy and Michael want to buy a mobile phone because (...).
....
....

e. (...) loves surfing on social media websites.
....
....

4 Participez à la conversation en vous servant des informations entre parenthèses.

a. Hey Sarah, what are you doing?

(Dites que vous êtes en train de poster une vidéo sur YouTube sur comment trouver le petit ami parfait !)

....

....

b. Really? Why don't you just create a blog?

(Dites que c'est trop compliqué et qu'aujourd'hui les gens préfèrent regarder des vidéos.)

....

....

c. Great! I think Shirley needs to watch your video then, doesn't she?

(Vous êtes d'accord car Shirley a des soucis avec son petit ami en ce moment. D'ailleurs elle dit qu'elle va le laisser tomber (= dump).

....

....

d. Really? So she definitely needs some tips to find Mr. Right.

(Vous répondez que oui et que c'est la raison pour laquelle vous postez cette vidéo sur la toile, pour l'aider elle et toutes les filles qui sont dans la même situation).

....

....

GRAMMAR

5 Vous décidez de créer un blog sur le site de votre lycée pour organiser la soirée de fin d'année de terminale et pouvoir communiquer avec tous les élèves.
Complétez cette affiche que vous placarderez dans le hall d'entrée avec les informations suivantes.

(a) nous allons créer un blog
(b) nous allons y mettre toutes nos idées
(c) je suis en train d'écrire
(d) un webmestre est déjà en train de créer
(e) ce que vous considérez important
(f) ce à quoi nous devons penser
(g) ce que nous ne voulons pas
(h) vous voulez vous impliquer dans l'organisation de cette fête
(i) nous allons tous nous réunir
(j) que nous allons transmettre

Hello everyone!

With a group of volunteers, (a) ....
to organise our annual party after our final exams.

(b) .... together
on that blog to share ideas on how to make that event memorable.

So while (c) .... this note
(d) .... the front page of our blog.

So, please send us your ideas about (e) .... not to
forget, (f) .... about, and
(g) .... , if (h) ....
....

After that, (i) ....
in the students' union centre on Thursday, October 6th at 12:00 to discuss
the ideas we have collected from that blog and make decisions (j) ....
.... to the principal.

The more you post, the more ideas we will have!

The Students' Union representatives

23

Exprimer des faits, des événements et des histoires au passé

Le prétérit simple / le prétérit en *be + V-ing*

IN A WORD

- Le **prétérit simple** exprime des actions et des faits passés, coupés du présent. Il sert aussi à raconter une histoire (passé de narration), une suite d'événements, et s'utilise avec des marqueurs temporels comme *ago, when, last year / month, yesterday, in 2019.*
  *I **went** to the USA for the first time ten years ago. I **didn't visit** the West Coast unfortunately.*

- Le **prétérit en *be + V-ing*** s'emploie avec **be** au passé (**was** ou **were**) à toutes les formes. Il exprime une action ou un événement en cours de déroulement à un moment précis dans le passé. Il peut servir de cadre, de décor à un autre événement dans le passé.
  *When I lived in the USA, I **was travelling** and **working** at the same time.*

⚠ ***Be + V-ing*** s'emploie très rarement avec les verbes d'état (*be, belong, seem,* etc.), de goût (*love, want,* etc.) et d'opinion (*think, consider,* etc.).

"We decided to get out and spend the kids'inheritance. Unfortunately they insisted on coming with us!"

---

1 **Mettez les verbes entre parenthèses au prétérit simple ou en *be + V-ing* en fonction du contexte.**
My sister and I (lose) our passports when we (drive) from the station to our hotel in Ottawa.
→ *My sister and I lost our passports when we were driving from the station to our hotel in Ottawa.*

a. .... (you know) that Patrick .... (study) at a university in London?

b. When Lisa and Thomas .... (decide) to give up everything to go to Australia, they .... (live) in Boston.

c. .... (they plan) to move to Ireland at that time?

d. Who .... (Karen contact) to apply for an *au pair* position?

e. Helen .... (really consider) making a world tour after her graduation.

f. Arthur's experience as a voluntourist in Bangladesh .... (not / turn out) to be be very rewarding for him.

g. .... (Sam and Esther work) as expatriates in India in the 90s?

2 **Créez les questions et les réponses au prétérit en *be + V-ing* avec les éléments suivants.**
A: What / the people on the seashore / look at?
B: the sunset.
A: What were the people on the seashore looking at?
B: They were looking at the sunset.

a. A: Who / the customs officer / talk to / ?   B: my sister
A: ....
....
B: ....
....

b. A: How / your grandparents / travel / to reach the continent / ?   B: by boat
A: ....
....
B: ....
....

c. A: What / the tourist guide / ask / that American family in front of us / ?   B: where they came from.
A: ....
....
B: ....
....

d. A: Why / you / wait / for your plane to take off?
B: because of a mechanical problem
A: ....
....
B: ....
....

e. A: Where / Sylvia and John / live when they asked for a Canadian visa ?   B: at John's parents'
A: ....
....
B: ....
....

f. A: Whose children / swim / in the pool when we arrived / ?
B: My sister's children
A: ....
....
B: ....
....

3 **Choisissez entre le prétérit simple et le prétérit en** *be + V-ing.*
I (be) really impressed by the huge buildings when I first (arrive) in New York. → *I was really impressed by the huge buildings when I first arrived in New York.*

a. Heather first .... (apply) for her tourist visa before she .... (decide) to apply for a work visa in Sydney, Australia.

b. My parents .... (be) very happy with my decision when I .... (tell) them that I .... (leave) for six months for a humanitarian project in Delhi.

c. Cassandra .... (read) a tourist guide about Scotland while I .... (watch) a TV documentary about the Loch Ness Monster.

d. I .... (not / want) to leave university for a gap year because I .... (wait) for an answer after my application to a medical school for the following year.

e. I .... (love) visiting Japan while the cherry trees .... (bloom).

4 **Vous revenez de votre séjour universitaire de six mois à Oxford. Vous écrivez une carte à un(e) ami(e) d'une autre nationalité pour lui raconter votre expérience. Complétez votre lettre avec les informations suivantes.**

(a) vous êtes revenu(e) d'Oxford la semaine dernière
(b) vous y avez passé six mois
(c) vous avez vraiment aimé votre séjour
(d) vous vous êtes fait de nombreux nouveaux amis de différents pays
(e) les professeurs parlaient assez lentement
(f) ils n'ont pas fait d'efforts particuliers lorsqu'ils parlaient
(g) certains d'entre eux vous parlaient
(h) ils disaient que vous faisiez des progrès (= *make progress*)
(i) ce qui fut le cas pour vous

Monday, October 1ˢᵗ

Hello!

(a) ....
where (b) ....
studying at the university.
(c) .... and
(d) ....
(e) ....
(f) .... but
....
(g) ....
at the end of their lessons.
(h) ....
very quickly and that we would probably succeed in our
final exams, (i) ....!

Thanks again for your advice. I am looking forward to seeing you soon to give you more details!

Hugs,
Sam

Faire le lien entre le passé et le présent

Le *present perfect*

bordas
Flash
PAGE
exercices
supplémentaires
interactifs

IN A WORD

- Le *present perfect* **simple** (*have / has* + **participe passé**) exprime des constats et des bilans dans le présent. *Banksy **has displayed** most of his work on publicly visible surfaces.*

- Le *present perfect* **en be + V-ing** (*have / has been* + *V-ing*) peut s'employer aussi pour exprimer une action qui a commencé dans le passé et qui est toujours en cours.
*Cindy Sherman **has been portraying** abstract female faces for a long time.*
Il met l'accent sur l'action ou sur le sujet de l'action.

⚠ – On utilise *for* pour indiquer une durée et *since* pour le point de départ d'une action :
*I **have loved** pop art **since** I was a teenager / **for** a long time.*

– On ne peut pas utiliser le *present perfect* quand les marqueurs de temps placent l'événement dans le passé (*one day ago*, *last month*, *yesterday*...).

– *Be + V-ing* s'emploie très rarement avec les verbes d'état (*be*, *belong*, *seem*, etc.), de goût (*love*, *want*, etc.) et d'opinion (*think*, *consider*, etc.).

1 Mettez les phrases suivantes au *present perfect* simple.
Jeff Koons's creative approach in Balloon Dog Blue *(trigger) many criticisms.*
→ *Jeff Koons's creative approach in* Balloon Dog Blue *has triggered many criticisms.*

a. One of David Hockney's paintings .... (recently / become) the world's most expensive painting, selling at $90 million.

b. .... British contemporary artist David Hockney .... (really / paint) Garden?

c. I .... (never / see) the American artist Edward Hopper's painting called *Nighthawks*.

d. Unfortunately, *ArtReview* magazine .... (not / rank) British painter Cecily Brown as one of the most influential contemporary artists in the world.

e. .... (African-American artist Kara Walker / not / deal with) the themes of racism and slavery in her illustrations?

f. British painter Iain Andrews .... (also / produce) the acrylic canvas called *Tiepolo's Stepmother*.

2 Imaginez ce qui vient de se passer au Metropolitan Museum of Art de New York et complétez ce dialogue en utilisant les verbes suivants au *present perfect* simple ou en *be + V-ing* selon la situation.
A : Look, Cindy Sherman's photographs (be removed)!
B : Yes, indeed. Visitors (ask) why they (be replaced) by Annie Leibovitz's.
→ *A : Look, Cindy Sherman's photographs have been removed! B : Yes, indeed. Visitors have been asking why they have been replaced by Annie Leibovitz's.*

a
A: Good morning Jack, how long .... (you / wait) in front of The Met?

B: I .... (wait) for 2 hours!

b
A: I .... (just / come out) of the museum. There .... (be) a huge problem: Mary Cassatt's painting called Young Mother Sewing .... (disappear)!

B: No way!

c

A: Yes, I know! All I can say is that a woman was screaming so loud that all the security guards .... (develop) headaches.

B: And what are they doing about it?

d

A: Well, everyone .... (calm down) now as you can see and the police .... (be called).

B: I see. .... (the police / arrive?) I can't see them...

e

A: No, they .... (not yet / arrive). The whole art section of the museum .... (just / be closed).

B: OK, I understand now why we .... (all / queue) for so long now...

GRAMMAR

3 **Vous interviewez un sculpteur et vidéaste américain célèbre pour le journal de votre lycée. Complétez le dialogue.**

a. You: "Good morning Sir, thank you so much for inviting me to your studio."

Artist: "You're welcome. Thank you for coming. I'm delighted to meet you."

b. You: *(Demandez depuis combien de temps il travaille en tant qu'artiste.)*
....
....

Artist: *(Il répond qu'il sculpte depuis son arrivée à San Francisco en 2005.)*
....
....

c. You: *(Demandez-lui pourquoi il a toujours été difficile de définir son style.)*
"Thank you. ....
....

Artist: *(Il répond qu'il pense que c'est parce qu'il a exploré différentes formes d'expression.)*
....
....

d. You: *(Demandez-lui sur quoi il se concentre depuis ces dernières années.)*
"And ....
....
....

Artist: *(Il dit que depuis qu'il est venu habiter à Paris, il se concentre davantage sur la réalisation de petits films et le dessin.)*
"Well, ...
....
....

e. You: "Thank you for answering my questions."

Artist: *(Il répond que ça a été un plaisir.)*
....

27

GRAMMAR

Exprimer des constats, des bilans et des événements antérieurs à d'autres événements passés

Le *past perfect*

Flash PAGE
exercices supplémentaires interactifs

IN A WORD

- Le *past perfect* simple (*had* + participe passé) exprime un événement antérieur à un autre événement passé. Il permet de faire le bilan à un moment précis dans le passé.
He suddenly realised he had forgotten to apply for a summer job.

- Le *past perfect* en *be + V-ing* (*had been + V-ing*) exprime un événement antérieur à un autre événement passé. Il met l'accent sur l'action ou sur le sujet de l'action. *She was tired because she had been serving tables all evening.* Il s'emploie très rarement avec les verbes d'état (*be, belong, seem,* etc.), de goût (*love, want,* etc.) et d'opinion (*think, consider,* etc.).

⚠️ 🇬🇧 On traduit le *past perfect* en *be + V-ing* par un imparfait en français si la durée de l'événement est indiquée : *He had been living in London for several weeks when he fell ill.* → Il vivait à Londres depuis plusieurs semaines lorsqu'il est tombé malade.

---

1 **Mettez les phrases suivantes au *past perfect* simple.**
Susan found work just two weeks after she (arrive) in New York. → *Susan found work just two weeks after she had arrived in New York.*

a. I realised when I saw her at the party in Dublin that we .... (already / work) together.

b. She told me that she .... (never / be) to Ireland before this summer job in Dublin.

c. We were on our way to the flat when I realised I .... (get) a text about a job.

d. Sue called Mike, who said that he .... (hand in) his suit to the laundry.

e. By the time Pete got back to work everyone .... (go) home.

2 **Formez des phrases avec les éléments suivants.**
I had worked – I bought – after – my plane tickets – all summer. → *I bought my plane tickets after I had worked all summer.*

a. wanted to work – he – once – on an Australian farm – he had seen the Australian landscape.
....
....

b. his English still wasn't fluent – as an *au pair* – although – for three months, – he had worked
....
....
....

c. I was 16 – by the time – many summer jobs – I had already had
....
....
....

d. since the age of 15 – as he had been to cooking school – how to cook – he knew
....
....

---

e. because – she had never worked as a waitress before – she was afraid – when she started working in a Scottish restaurant
....
....
....

3 **Vous travaillez dans un café. Votre patron britannique souhaite embaucher un(e) étudiant(e). Il vous charge de lui faire un compte-rendu du CV et de la lettre de motivation de Jeanne Dupont, une étudiante française. Traduisez-lui les informations suivantes.**

Notes on Jeanne Dupont's biography:

(a) Elle est née le 6 décembre 1998 à Bordeaux. ....
....

(b) Cela faisait trois ans qu'elle étudiait la traduction à l'université d'Angers quand elle a décidé de s'installer à Tours, en 2019. ....
....
....

(c) Elle avait toujours voulu voyager donc en 2020 elle a décidé de déménager en Angleterre. ....
....
....

(d) Elle travaillait depuis trois mois quand elle a vu l'annonce. ....
....

(e) Elle pensait que son anglais s'était amélioré depuis son arrivée et que son français pourrait être utile dans un café. ....
....

Exprimer des prévisions, des événements planifiés, des intentions

L'expression du futur

 Pour exprimer le futur en anglais, on peut utiliser :
- **will / won't + BV** pour une simple prédiction ou une décision prise au moment où l'on parle :
  *A new gender wage equality law **will be** implemented.*
- **be going to + BV** pour une intention ou conviction (indices permettant de faire le pronostic) :
  *The riot police **are going to march** towards the demonstrators, they're lifting their shields.*
- **be about to + BV** pour un futur très proche : *The demonstration **is about to start**.*
- **be to + BV** pour des événements planifiés : *The union leader **is to make** a speech on Thursday.*
- **be sure to + BV** pour exprimer une certitude :
  *Women **are sure to fight** for wage equality in the coming months.*

GRAMMAR

1 Entourez les expressions en gras les plus appropriées selon le contexte.
Amanda (is sure to) / is about to *win her case against her abusive employer if she goes to court.*

a. Next week, women **will / are going to** demonstrate to keep their retirement rights.

b. Look, some people **are about to / are to** start a sit-in!

c. The laws against discrimination **are sure to / will** evolve since Parliament is currently debating that issue.

d. The leader of the demonstration **is to / is about to** make a speech at the end of the day, the stage is already prepared.

e. If women don't fight for their rights, they **won't / aren't to** get the same executive job opportunities as men.

2 Traduisez les éléments manquants pour compléter les phrases suivantes.
The president (va défendre) her point of view.
→ *The president is going to defend her point of view.*

a. Parliament .... (*est sur le point de*) vote a law to guarantee equal opportunities for women.

b. .... (*Je suis sûr(e) d'aller manifester*) for gender equality this afternoon.

c. .... (*Je ferai*) the best speech ever to defend women's rights!

d. .... (*Il est prévu que les étudiants manifestent*) at 4:00 p.m. today to show their support.

e. In the coming days, the State Secretary for Equal Opportunities .... (*va parler*) a law that guarantees financial aid for students who are single parents.

3 Vous écrivez à un député pour lui faire part de vos inquiétudes dans le cadre d'une future réforme du système éducatif. Complétez ce que vous lui dites.

(a) Je vais vous dire ce qui m'inquiète
(b) certaines personnes seront désavantagées
(c) sont sûres d'avoir moins d'options
(d) vous êtes sur le point de discuter
(e) Les voix des élèves sont à prendre en considération
(f) ils ne se laisseront pas faire (= *let themselves be pushed around*)
(g) exprimeront leur colère (= *anger*) dans la rue

October 22ⁿᵈ

Dear Member of Parliament,

(a) ....
about the new education reform. I'm afraid that
(b) .... .

They (c) ....
when choosing their subjects.

Therefore, since (d) ....
education reforms in Parliament next month, we would like you to defend our rights to a full and diverse education.

(e) ....
.... in your parliament debates.
If not, (f) ....
.... and (g) ....

Yours sincerely,

Anna Walker

Poser des questions, confirmer, infirmer

La forme interrogative

 **IN A WORD**

- Les questions en **wh-** (questions ouvertes) commencent par un mot interrogatif.
  When did India become an independent nation?
  How many people live in New Delhi today?

- Les **yes / no questions** (questions fermées) commencent par un auxiliaire.
  Have you ever been to Australia?

- L'ordre des mots est le même dans les **yes / no questions** et les **wh- questions** : auxiliaire + sujet + verbe.

⚠ Si la question porte sur le sujet, il n'y a pas d'inversion du sujet : *Who is the Governor of Canada?*

"DOES YOUR DOG BITE?"

❶ Complétez les phrases ci-dessous par le pronom interrogatif qui convient.

A: ... was the president of the United States of America in 1962? B: It was John Fitzgerald Kennedy.
→ A: Who was the president of the United States of America in 1962?

a. A: .... was there a Civil War between 1861 and 1865 in the United States? B: Because there were economic and ideological rivalries between the North and the South.

b. A: .... have you been to Scotland? B: I have only been twice.

c. A: .... civilians were killed during the Bloody Sunday events on January 30th 1972 in Northern Ireland? B: There were 14 in all.

d. A: .... will the presidential plane land at? B: Air Force One is expected to land at 1:35 p.m. local time.

e. A: .... was the candidate standing against Donald Trump during the 2016 presidential campaign in the US? B: I think it was Democrat Hillary Clinton.

f. A: .... will the European Union accept a new country member? B: Well, I don't know. A few countries are presently applying but no date has been set.

g. A: .... money does NASA invest in its 2020 space programme? B: I have heard that it is $21 billion for the 2020 fiscal year.

h. A: .... exactly did Armstrong and Aldrin land on July 20th, 1969? B: They landed on the moon, in the Sea of Tranquility.

❷ Remettez les éléments dans l'ordre pour poser des questions ouvertes ou fermées.

London – Pamela – does – how – ? – to – go – often
→ How often does Pamela go to London?

a. going – when – are – to – Glasgow – ? – your parents
....

b. ? – you – and – between – do – Northern Ireland – country – Wales – which – prefer
....

c. don't – believe – ? – you – can become – that – an independent country – Scotland
....
....

d. be traveling – will – next – holidays – for – you – your – Jamaica – ? – to
....
....

e. the British economy – who – Brexit – the consequences – of – ? – knows – on
....
....

❸ Retrouvez les questions qui portent sur les éléments soulignés.

How tall was President Abraham Lincoln?
→ President Abraham Lincoln was 1.93 m tall.

a. ....
The current wall between the USA and Mexico is 1,052 km long from Texas to California.

b. ....
One World Trade Center is currently the highest building in the USA, it is 541 m high.

c. ....
....
US President Abraham Lincoln was 59 when he was assassinated in Washington D.C. on April 15th, 1865.

d. ....
The Unites States of America is 4,506 kilometers wide from east to west.

e. ....
Lake Tahoe is 501 m deep.

f. ....
The Statue of Liberty is 93 m high.

4 Vous interviewez un(e) étudiant(e) irlandais(e) de retour après un échange Erasmus+. Complétez ce dialogue.

a. "Good evening, and welcome to our programme. Tonight we welcome a student who experienced an Erasmus+ exchange programme. (*Vous demandez si un tel échange est bénéfique.*)

....
....

"Yes, it is. Spending six months abroad is a wonderful experience!"

b. "This is what our programme is going to be about! (*Vous demandez si chaque étudiant devrait saisir* (= take) *l'occasion de vivre dans un autre pays un certain temps.*)

....
....
....

"Yes, I really think they should. I even consider it should be compulsory when you follow a university education."

c. "(Vous demandez pourquoi.)

....
....

"Well, if we want to open up to the world and discover new cultures and new people before starting our professional life, it is the best moment to do so, isn't it?"

d. "Not necessarily. (*Vous demandez si ce n'est pas mieux de prendre une année sabbatique* (= gap year) *à la fin de vos études.*)

....
....
....

"Yes, perhaps, but when you have personal and family responsibilities, it can be much more difficult to leave."

5 Vous êtes un(e) fervent(e) partisan(e) des programmes Erasmus+. On vous embauche pour en faire la promotion. On vous charge de rédiger un prospectus que vous distribuerez à la sortie des établissements scolaires. Faites-y figurer les questions suivantes.

a. Êtes-vous prêt(e) à voyager ?

b. Souhaiteriez-vous bouger au sein de l'Union européenne ?

c. Voulez-vous vivre de merveilleuses expériences culturelles ?

d. Ne voulez-vous pas avoir davantage de liberté ?

e. Serez-vous prêt(e) à changer votre style de vie pendant six mois ?

Erasmus+

ENROLL IN OUR ERASMUS+ PROGRAMMES!

a. ....

b. ....
....

c. ....
....

d. ....

e. ....
....

Exprimer la capacité, l'obligation, la permission, le conseil et leurs contraires

Les auxiliaires modaux – sens 1

 **IN A WORD**

Les **auxiliaires modaux (sens 1)** expriment :

- la capacité (*I* **can** *speak English.* / *He* **couldn't** *understand the problem.*)
- l'interdiction (*They* **mustn't** *exclude anyone.* / *They* **can't** *leave the classroom.*)
- la permission (*You* **may** / **can** *come in.* **Might** / **Could** *I come with you?*)
- l'obligation (*You* **must** *take notes.*) ou l'absence d'obligation (*You* **needn't** *get up early.*)
- le conseil (*You* **should** *revise.*)

Les modaux sont toujours suivis d'une base verbale. On utilise un équivalent lorsqu'un modal n'est utilisable qu'au présent (**must** / **can** / **may**).

⚠ On ne peut avoir deux modaux à la suite. Au besoin, on utilise une équivalence.

"This time X is 7. Last time it was 4. And the time before that it was 12. Maybe X should take some time to reflect and decide for itself what it really wants to be."

---

1 **Complétez les phrases avec un modal à l'aide des indications entre parenthèses.**
He (...) talk to the headmaster about the problem. (obligation)
→ *He must talk to the headmaster about the problem.*

a. You really .... take into account the different points of view. *(conseil)*

b. He .... feel so bad about the situation as he is not alone. *(absence d'obligation)*

c. I will tell them that they .... exclude anyone from the activity. *(interdiction)*

d. Do you think she .... learn from her mistakes? *(capacité)*

e. Whatever I do, I .... keep my cool. *(obligation)*

f. You .... leave your skateboard here as it blocks the path. *(interdiction)*

2 **Construisez des phrases à partir des éléments donnés.**
he – he – is – on the phone – ? – always shout – must – when
→ *Must he always shout when he is on the phone?*

a. you – if you – to walk up the stairs – use the lift – shouldn't – are able

b. wheelchair accessible – must – every school – that it is – make sure

c. if there aren't – build a ramp – needn't – any stairs – schools

d. be – could – as a day without meat – lunches – vegetarian once a week – is healthy

e. students – by visiting the website – learn – can – about the school's inclusion policy

3 **Reformulez les phrases en utilisant un auxiliaire modal.**
I advise you to speak up against bullying.
→ *You should speak up against bullying.*

a. Students are allowed to organise meetings in the school hall.

b. They don't have to invite teachers unless they want to.

c. They have to book the school hall in advance.

d. Students are forbidden to eat in the school hall during the meeting.

e. However, they are allowed to bring water to the meeting.

4 Créez une affiche pour favoriser l'inclusion dans votre lycée.
Complétez avec des conseils en variant les auxiliaires modaux utilisés.

a. ....

b. ....

c. ....

d. ....

e. ....

f. ....

5 The Halloween party!

a. Participez à la conversation en vous servant des informations entre parenthèses.
Utilisez l'auxiliaire modal approprié.

1. Our class is organising a party for Halloween.

(Demandez si vous pouvez y aller.)
....
....

2. Yes, of course you can! By the way, there's a new student in our class.

(Suggérez qu'on l'invite à la fête.)
....
....

3. Good idea. We can invite the whole year. Would the school hall be big enough?

(Vous pensez que vous pourriez aussi demander d'utiliser la cantine.)
....
....

4. I'll do that. Do you think we should prepare invitations?

(D'après vous, il n'est pas nécessaire de faire des invitations mais on pourrait utiliser le site web du lycée pour informer tout le monde.)
....
....

5. Yes, why not? What about disguises?

(Vous adorez cette idée et vous pensez qu'on doit absolument l'adopter.)
....
....

b. **Vous devez poster un message d'invitation sur le site du lycée. Appuyez-vous sur le contexte ci-dessous.**

Vous avez décidé d'organiser une soirée.
Venez déguisé(e). Tous les déguisements sont possibles. Soyez original(e).
Et si vous savez danser, participez au concours de danse. Vous pouvez venir seul(e) ou accompagné(e) d'un(e) ami(e).

Q f ♥ ✉ Login | Register 👤

Hi everyone!

So, we've decided to .... at the school hall next month.

If you want to come you are welcome but you..

You .... any disguise you like... but you

.... as there will be a prize for the best one.

And if you think you ....

.... You .... of course, but you

.... if you want to.

More details will be posted soon.
Have a great day!

Exprimer les degrés de probabilité d'un événement présent, passé ou futur

Les auxiliaires modaux – sens 2

> **IN A WORD**
>
> ● Les **auxiliaires modaux (sens 2)** expriment la probabilité. Selon les degrés de probabilité, on peut utiliser :
> - **can't** (quasi impossible = possible à 10 % : *It can't be true.*),
> - **might / could** (possible à 25 % : *He might / could be the killer.*),
> - **may** (probable à 50 % : *They may have a good motive*), et
> - **must** (quasi certain = possible à 80 % : *The victim must be dead.*).
>
> ● Au présent, les modaux sont toujours suivis d'une base verbale (**infinitif sans to**).
>
> ⚠ – Pour un événement passé, on utilise la structure : **modal (+ not) + have + participe passé** :
> *The killer **may (not) have escaped** through the window, it **must have been** someone who had the door key.*
>
> – Un modal peut également s'exprimer avec des adverbes et des expressions équivalentes comme par exemple pour **may** : *it's possible that, perhaps, maybe, probably, it's (very) likely that...*

❶ Complétez les phrases avec un modal et adaptez les verbes à l'aide des indications entre parenthèses.
I saw Jane yesterday, she was fine! What you are telling me ... (be) true! (quasi impossible dans le présent) → *I saw Jane yesterday, she was fine! What you are telling me can't be true!*

a. The judge .... (summon) Sir Andrew to explain what he did yesterday between 10:00 p.m. and midnight. *(possible à 25 %)*

b. The mystery remains but Jack the Ripper

.... (be) Polish barber Aaron Kosminski. *(possible dans le passé à 50 %)*

c. Deirdre .... (be suspected), she loved her deceased husband so much! *(quasi impossible)*

d. The neighbours .... (hear) gun shots last night. *(quasi certain dans le passé à 80 %)*

e. The police .... (investigate) the case. *(possible à 50 %)*

❷ Formez des phrases en remettant les éléments dans l'ordre.
UFOs – have – some people – the lights – been – think – in the sky – might – they saw →*Some people think the lights they saw in the sky might have been UFOs.*

a. some DNA samples – must – collected – have been – on the murder scene – there.

....

....

b. from Alcatraz – escaped – who – have – in the icy water of the Pacific – can't – the prisoners – survived

....

....

c. have – The Mary Celeste ship – attacked – in 1872 – might – the eight people on board – been – by pirates

....

....

d. where – is located in the desert of Nevada – be – are kept – a secret base – Area 51 – crashed UFOs – and could

....

❸ Reformulez les probabilités en utilisant un auxiliaire modal.
It's impossible that you didn't hear the noise the burglars made upstairs! → *You must have heard the noise the burglars made upstairs!*

a. Never forget that maybe your daughter is lying to you...

....

....

b. It's almost certain that Bryan stole the silver cutlery, he looks so embarrassed!

....

....

c. It is possible that my brother will have problems with the police if he doesn't tell them what he knows.

....

....

d. There is a little hope that the police find out one day who the "Zodiac Killer" really was.

....

....

e. It's impossible that the Malaysian Airlines Boeing 777 landed safely after it suddenly vanished from the radars on March 8th, 2014.

....

....

4 **Vous êtes commissaire de police. Après la découverte de trois cadavres dans les allées de Central Park, vous rédigez une note synthétique à l'attention de l'enquêteur en chef pour lui exposer les premières constatations et hypothèses sur ce qui se serait passé.**
Appuyez-vous sur votre brouillon. Utilisez des auxiliaires de modalité.

Your draft (= votre brouillon):

Central Park murder case investigation. January 7, 2020

a. *Almost certain that the three victims killed between 10:00 p.m. and midnight → state of the corpses.*

b. *Hole in the iron fence at the entrance of the park → Killer perhaps got into park through that hole.*

c. *Three bodies found in three different areas of park + IDs show they are perhaps not family-related.*

d. *Purses, watches, wallets, jewels still present on crime scene → killer probably not interested in money (no theft).*

e. *Same killer almost for sure → throats slashed with same knife (identical wounds on the three victims).*

```
New York Central Police Department
Murder case investigation nb.: 67
Place: Central Park, NY
Date: January 7, 2020
Officer: M. Hector Smithlane

First hypothetical conclusions:
a.
..................................................
..................................................
b.
..................................................
..................................................
..................................................
```

```
c.
..................................................
..................................................
..................................................
                                              .
d.
..................................................
..................................................
                                              .
e.
..................................................
..................................................
..................................................
                                              .
```

```
                              Hector Smithlane
```

5 **Suite à ces crimes, le commissariat central de New York vous demande de rédiger une courte note qui sera placardée sur les trois scènes de crime afin de retrouver de potentiels témoins et mettre en garde les promeneurs. Indiquez-y les éléments suivants.**

(a) Nous nous excusons pour la gêne que cette fermeture (= *closure*) peut occasionner.

(b) Il se pourrait que vous vous soyez promené(e) à cet endroit ou aux alentours dans la soirée du 7 janvier.

(c) Si c'est le cas, votre aide peut être utile.

(d) Si vous avez vu ou entendu quelque chose d'inhabituel ce soir-là, appelez le 0 800 911 911.

(e) Nous vous remercions pour toute aide que vous pourrez fournir.

NEW YORK CENTRAL POLICE DEPARTMENT

WARNING NOTE

Place: Central Park, NY

Dear walkers,

These areas of the park will be temporarily closed.

(a) ....
....

(b) ....
....
....

(c) ....
....

(d) ....
....
....

(e) ....
....

Désigner des éléments particuliers et des notions générales

Les articles

bordas
Flash
PAGE

exercices
supplémentaires
interactifs

• Il existe trois types d'articles en anglais : *a / an*, *the* et Ø (article zéro).
– *a / an* sert à désigner un élément sans le distinguer des autres :
*I'd rather go on **a** tour of **a** capital city than on **an** adventure track in the desert.*

– *the* désigne un élément spécifique connu de tous ou pour lequel le contexte apporte des précisions :
***The** rock climbing experience we had in Australia last winter was fabulous!*

– Ø s'utilise pour parler d'une notion en général ou d'un groupe tout entier :
Ø Bungee jumping is the scariest experience I've ever had.

⚠ ***A*** s'utilise devant un son consonne, ***an*** devant un son voyelle (*a gap year, an adventure*). Pour les noms propres, on dit: *Ø Prince Harry, Ø Australia*, mais : ***the** Netherlands* ou ***the** USA* car ces pays sont au pluriel.

IRONICALLY, IT WASN'T JUST THE SCEPTICS OR THE ANTI-CLIMATE MOVEMENT THAT OBSTRUCTED CLIMATE CHANGE RESEARCH...

---

1 Complétez les phrases avec les articles *a / an, the* ou Ø.

I'm afraid of (...) airplanes. I'm going to take (...) sleeping pill during (...) flight. → *I'm afraid of Ø airplanes. I'm going to take a sleeping pill during the flight.*

a. After my exams I've decided to take .... one-year break to travel around .... world.

b. Going to .... Australia has always been .... dream for my parents and my sister.

c. .... road trip we did last year in the West of .... USA was wonderful.

d. Karen had .... courage to jump from .... airplane with .... parachute!

e. Sometimes .... gap year students don't go back to .... college upon their return.

2  Traduisez les phrases suivantes.

a. L'année dernière, mon frère a eu l'opportunité d'aller en Nouvelle-Zélande. Quelle aventure !

....

....

b. Quand j'aurai le temps de voyager, j'irai en Écosse. J'aime la randonnée (= *hiking*) dans la campagne écossaise.

....

....

....

c. Les immeubles de New York me donnent le vertige (= *vertigo*).

....

d. Les gens sont parfois inquiets lorsqu'ils prennent l'avion.

....

....

e. Le volontourisme (= *voluntourism*) est une mode qui offre l'opportunité d'aider les gens.

....

....

3 Vous êtes à Perth en Australie pour six mois. Vous écrivez à vos parents. Complétez la lettre.

(a) Le vol / à l'aéroport de Perth

(b) Les gens / un couple de retraités (= *retired*)

(c) Ils habitent dans une ferme incroyablement grande avec beaucoup d'animaux

(d) les kangourous / librement dans la ferme / peur des humains

(e) de la nourriture / des animaux nuisibles (= *pests*) / les cultures (= *crops*)

(f) les kangourous / la ferme

(g) une mission très difficile / mes amis / une photo !

Perth, June 22

Dear mum and dad,

I hope that you are both fine. I am finally taking the time to write to you.

(a) .... I took was delayed but I arrived safely .... (b) ....
I live with are John and Sheila, ...
(c) ....
.... around them. (d)
What is incredible is that ....
jump around .... and are not at all
.... (e) It's because they are
looking for .... But here they are considered
.... because they destroy ....
(f) I find .... adorable, but
I was hired to keep them away from ....
(g) It's going to be ....
because they are already ....
I'll send you ....

I'll write to you again soon.
Take care,

Sam

Les dénombrables et les indénombrables

- Il existe des noms que l'on peut compter, les **dénombrables**, comme *car, house, person* et des noms que l'on ne peut pas compter, les **indénombrables**, comme *water, money, furniture, advice, information, luggage*.

- Les **dénombrables** prennent l'article ***the / a / an***, ils peuvent se mettre au singulier ou au pluriel (régulier avec **s** ou irrégulier) et peuvent être précédés d'un nombre : *Two children*.

- Les **indénombrables** désignent une idée ou une notion abstraite, des matériaux, des aliments ou un ensemble : *You need Ø money*. Ils ne peuvent être précédés de l'article ***a / an*** ou d'un nombre. Ils sont toujours au singulier et sont suivis d'un verbe à la 3ᵉ personne du singulier : *Your luggage is heavy!* On peut les compter avec des expressions comme *a piece of (advice), a loaf / slice of (bread)*.

⚠️ On dit : *Ø people are* (= les gens sont) mais *a people* (= un peuple). *Ø hair* (= cheveux) mais *a hair* (= un poil). Certains mots qui se terminent par un **s** sont invariables (*the news is… – an endangered species needs …*). Pour dire « une information », il faut dire : *a piece of information*.

1 Classez les mots suivants selon qu'ils sont dénombrables ou indénombrables. Vérifiez dans un dictionnaire si vous avez des doutes.

| boat | – | money | – | knowledge | – | plane | – | evidence |
| wave | – | baggage | – | bungalow |

Dénombrables　　　　　　**Indénombrables**

2 Utilisez l'article approprié selon que le nom est dénombrable (*the / a*) ou indénombrable (*Ø*).

I love (…) chocolate. → *I love Ø chocolate.*

a. Sylvia and John brought back .... cheese when they went on a trip to .... Netherlands.

b. .... plane I took to fly from .... San Francisco to .... Los Angeles was late, as there was .... storm.

c. I would like you to give me .... advice on all .... places to visit in .... New York.

d. I hate .... rice and when we went to .... Asia my mom went crazy as I wanted to eat .... hamburger.

3 Traduisez les phrases suivantes en utilisant l'article approprié.

a. J'ai besoin d'informations, où puis-je trouver une carte de la ville ?

b. J'adore les meubles asiatiques. Mark et moi en avons rapporté quelques-uns du Japon.

c. Sam et Sheila hésitent à faire une randonnée (= *to go on a trek*) dans le désert de la vallée de la Mort à cause de la chaleur le jour et du froid la nuit.

d. As-tu de l'argent pour payer une croisière (= *cruise*) d'une semaine dans les Bahamas ?

4 Vous êtes à Perth en Australie pour six mois. Vous écrivez à vos parents. Complétez la lettre.

(a) Les gens sont très gentils
(b) si j'ai besoin d'informations ou d'aide
(c) la nourriture est délicieuse
(d) je mange de la viande tous les jours
(e) le mobilier
(f) je dois rencontrer un ami

May 21ˢᵗ, 2020

Hi everyone!

Hope you're all doing well and missing me like a toothache, ha, ha. Perth is totally cool. (a) .... I just have to look lost and I'm asked (b) ....

What else? Yeah, (c) ...., like, really awesome, (d) ....

The place I'm staying is cool too, (e) .... looks like something granny would love, but whatever.

Ok, gotta go, (f) ....

Love to all and Skype soon,

Sam

GRAMMAR

GRAMMAR

Désigner des quantités plus ou moins importantes
Les quantifieurs

bordas
Flash PAGE
exercices supplémentaires interactifs

IN A WORD

Les **quantifieurs** varient en fonction de la quantité que l'on souhaite exprimer et du type de nom :
- Rien / aucun(e) : **no** ou **none of** : *No* computer is…, ***none of** them is…*
- Peu de : **few** + **dénombrable** : *Few persons* (***little***) + indénombrable (sans **s**) : *Little warning*
- Quelques-un(e)s / un peu de : **a few** + **dénombrable** : *A few firewalls*, ou **a little** + **indénombrable** : *A little care*
- Un certain nombre, une certaine quantité : **some** + **dénombrable** : *some hackers*, ou **some** + **indénombrable** : *some advice*
- Beaucoup : **many / plenty of / a lot of / lots of** + **dénombrable** : *many websites*, ou **much / plenty of / a lot of / lots of** + **indénombrable** : *lots of information*.
- Beaucoup trop : **too many** + **dénombrable** : *too many websites*, ou **too much** + **indénombrable** : *too much information*

⚠️ 🇬🇧 Ne confondez pas l'adjectif *little* (petit) et le quantifieur *little* (peu) ou *a little* (un peu). De même, faites la différence entre *few* (peu de) et *a few* (quelques-un(e)s).

① Entourez le quantifieur approprié.

a little / ~~few~~ / none of web corporations respect our private data.

a. Many / much / a little teenagers think that putting **many / some** personal data on their websites will have **much / no** consequences.

b. Lots of / much / little corporations have adopted open space areas and not **a few / many / little** CEOs realise the lack of privacy it represents for the workers.

c. Paula feels **a few / few / a little** apprehension that when she surfs on the web there is **many / a lot of** danger that **few / many / none** hackers may have access to her data.

d. The Second Amendment of the US Constitution allows people to carry **no / some / none / few** guns, so **little / few / a few** is done to prevent people from buying one.

e. Few / none / none of the web giants have signed an agreement not to use people's private information.

② 🇬🇧 Complétez les traductions suivantes.

a. Peu de bureaux sont aménagés pour accueillir un(e) seul(e) employé(e). Souvent, il y a trop de personnes dans une pièce.

……………………………………… are designed to welcome only

one employee. There are often ……………………………………

………………………………………………………………………….

b. Beaucoup d'appartements modernes n'ont plus de stores (= *blinds*) aux fenêtres. Cela expose beaucoup trop nos vies privées.

…………………………………………………………no longer

……………………………………………………………………That

exposes our …………………………………………………………….

c. De nombreuses entreprises prennent des stagiaires (= *interns*).

…………………………………………………………………………

take on ………………………………………………….

③ Complétez le courriel avec ces éléments.

(a) de nombreux ordinateurs / beaucoup de documents confidentiels

(b) aucun(e) d'entre nous

(c) certain(e)s d'entre vous / quelques / beaucoup de détails

(d) une grande inquiétude (= *concern*) / certains de vos contacts externes

(e) aucune solution n'a été trouvée

(f) très peu d'informations importantes

New message ___ ⤢ ✕

From C. Tyson

To | All employees | Date | February 10 |

Subject | Protection of professional and personal data |

Dear collaborators,

I am writing to inform you that you must be very cautious about the emails you exchange. Our Intranet protection software was cracked

yesterday and (a) …………………………………………………………

containing …………………………………………………………………

……………………………………………… have been hacked.

So, (b) …………………………………………… is safe from being spied currently on.

If (c) ……………………………… have already been contacted by

……………………… so-called customers who ask you for ……………

……………………………………………………… about our structure, do not answer.

(d) There is also ……………………………………………………………

………………………………………… about the emails that you may

have sent to ………………………………………………………………,

their email addresses may have been hacked too.

Please inform them.

For the moment, (e) ……………………………………………………, so

(f) …………………………………………………… must be exchanged until the problem is solved.

I hope these guidelines will help us protect our private and professional data.

Kind regards,

C. Tyson

Send   A 📎 ⊙ ☺ 🖼   ⋮ 🗑

Comparer des éléments
Les comparatifs et les superlatifs

IN A WORD

Il existe plusieurs degrés de comparaison.
- Le comparatif de supériorité :
  - pour les adjectifs courts, on ajoute **-er à l'adjectif + than** : *faster than before*
  - pour les adjectifs longs, on utilise **more + adj. + than** : *more dangerous than before*
- Le comparatif d'égalité et d'inégalité : quelle que soit la longueur de l'adjectif, on utilise **(not) as + adj. + as** : *(not) as fascinating as*
- Le comparatif d'infériorité : quelle que soit la longueur de l'adjectif, on utilise **less + adj. + than** : *less innovative than*
- Le superlatif de supériorité :
  - pour les adjectifs courts : **the + adj. + -est** : *the biggest*
  - pour les adjectifs longs : **the most + adj.** : *the most useful*
- Le superlatif d'infériorité : quelle que soit la longueur de l'adjectif, on utilise **the least + adj.** : *the least impressive*

⚠️ Un adjectif court est un adjectif composé d'une syllabe (*tall*) ou de deux syllabes s'il se termine par **-er** (*clever*), **-ow** (*shallow*), **-y** (*pretty*) ou **-le** (*noble*). Tous les autres adjectifs sont longs.
Certains adjectifs sont irréguliers : **good – better – best ; bad – worse – worst ; far – further – furthest**.

❶ Faites une phrase en mettant l'adjectif entre parenthèses au comparatif de supériorité (+), d'égalité (=), d'inégalité (≠) ou d'infériorité (–).

Our responsibility in the medical field (= important) / in technological innovation.
→ *Our responsibility in the medical field is as important as in technological innovation.*

a. The progress in medicine (= fascinating) / the progress in new technologies.

....

....

b. The cloning of animals (– acceptable) / the cloning of plants in terms of ethics.

....

....

c. The treatment against breast cancer in 2020 (+ effective) / in the 1970s.

....

....

d. Research has helped us to understand outer space (+ good) / before.

....

....

❷ Complétez les phrases avec un superlatif de supériorité (+) ou d'infériorité (–).

Vocal information assistance is (+ important) progress made these last five years.
→ *Vocal information assistance is the most important progress made these last five years.*

a. Molecular cuisine is .... (+ incredible) innovation in cooking.

b. Humanoid receptionists that replace the front desk staff are .... (+ creepy) inventions.

c. Robot-assisted surgeries are .... (– costly) innovations to make surgeries less invasive.

d. Touch-screen tables are .... (+ funny) gadgets that I have ever seen.

❸ Complétez le début de cette interview.

a. Good morning, I'm honored to be able to interview (*une des ingénieures les plus célèbres*) ....

.... in robotics of our country. Thank you for accepting to answer our questions.

(*Elle vous répond qu'elle essaiera de donner les réponses les plus claires possibles.*)

Well, I will try to give .... answers.

b. OK, (*vous lui demandez ce qui est pour elle le plus gros défi*) .... in creating an artificial arm or leg that someone has lost?

Well, the technical aspect is (*elle répond que l'aspect technique est moins important pour elle que de convaincre les patients*) ....

.... that their life will be better with an artificial limb. (*Elle ajoute que c'est ça le défi le plus motivant !*) ....

c. I see. But what a satisfaction it must be for someone to get his or her arm or leg mobility back, don't you think?

Yes, indeed. (*Elle répond qu'elle en est aussi heureuse que la personne qu'elle aide.*) I must say

(*Cela fait partie des moments les plus magnifiques dans la vie.*) .... in life.

GRAMMAR

39

Présenter un fait en changeant de point de vue, utiliser la tournure impersonnelle « on »

La voix passive

bordas
Flash PAGE
exercices supplémentaires interactifs

 **IN A WORD**

- La voix passive se construit avec l'auxiliaire **be** (au temps de la phrase) et le verbe au **participe passé** (beaucoup de verbes sont irréguliers, il faut les connaître par cœur).
- On l'utilise quand on **s'intéresse** plutôt à la **personne** ou à **l'objet** qui subit l'action, au **résultat** de cette action et non à celui qui fait l'action (l'agent).

Voix active : *The Second Amendment of the US Constitution allows guns in the USA.*
→ Voix passive : *Guns **are allowed** in the USA by the Second Amendment of the US Constitution.*

- L'élément mis en avant devient alors le sujet du verbe et l'agent est souvent omis. S'il a une importance particulière, il est introduit par **by**.

⚠ Le passif sert aussi à traduire le « on » français. *People **were given** the right to carry weapons.*
→ On a donné le droit aux gens de porter des armes.

---

1 **Complétez les phrases avec le verbe proposé à la voix passive et au temps indiqué.**

Decide / simple past : A ceasefire (...) between General Grant and General Lee during the Secession War
→ A ceasefire was decided between General Grant and General Lee during the Secession War.

a. Shoot / present perfect: Oh no! A man ....

b. Interview / present + V-*ing*: Look, the President ....
.... on Channel 4 about the carrying of firearms.

c. Carry / simple present: Today in the US, over 98 million guns .... by civilians.

d. Disarm / simple past: Fortunately the student ....
.... by his classmates before he could use his rifle.

e. Sentence / future: I am sure the murderer ....
.... to life imprisonment by the jury.

2 **Réécrivez les phrases à la voix passive en mettant en avant les <u>éléments soulignés</u>.**

Anti-gun groups highly criticise <u>the National Rifle Association (NRA)</u>.
→ The NRA is highly criticised by anti-gun groups.

a. People buy <u>guns</u> all over the country.

....

b. They should take <u>drastic measures</u> to limit the sale of weapons to young adults.

....

c. The president of the NRA will hold a <u>speech</u> to defend our rights.

....

d. Many senators said that they would do <u>something</u> to reduce crimes due to weapons.

....

e. They assassinated <u>two Kennedy brothers</u> in the 1960s.

....
....

3 **Vous allez manifester dans les rues contre le port d'armes aux USA. Préparez un panneau sur lequel vous inscrirez les éléments suivants.**

(a) L'année dernière, 40 000 personnes ont été tuées par balle (= *firearms*).

(b) Chaque jour dans notre pays, 58 000 pistolets (= *handguns*) sont vendus.

(c) D'ici la semaine prochaine, 255 personnes seront abattues (= *shoot*) par arme à feu.

(d) Ne dites pas que rien ne peut être fait !

STOP GUN VIOLENCE IN OUR COUNTRY!

(a) ....
....

(b) ....
....

(c) ....
....

(d) ....

STOP GUN VIOLENCE

DON'T BUY GUNS!

La proposition relative

> **IN A WORD**
>
> ● La **proposition relative** apporte une information supplémentaire sur l'antécédent. Elle est introduite par un pronom relatif : *The food **that** you have not eaten can be used.*
>
> ● La nature de l'antécédent (humain ou non humain) et la fonction du pronom relatif (sujet ou complément) déterminent le choix du pronom relatif :
> – antécédent humain : on emploie **who** quand le pronom relatif est sujet et **who(m)**, **that** ou **Ø** quand il est complément : *Volunteers **who** serve during Christmas meal distributions are appreciated*.
> – antécédent non humain : on emploie **which** ou **that** quand le pronom relatif est sujet, ou **which**, **that** ou **Ø** s'il est complément : *The food **that / which** is wasted could be given to charities **that / which / Ø** / everyone knows like* Food Cycle.

GRAMMAR

❶ Complétez les phrases avec le pronom relatif qui convient.

The food (...) I don't eat gets systematically frozen.
→ *The food that / which / Ø I don't eat gets systematically frozen.*

a. The people........................I talked to told me they were shocked by the amount of food that is wasted.

b. A law .... forbids supermarkets to throw away unsold food has helped reduce waste.

c. The Danish,.......................care more than many about recycling food, are an example to follow.

d. The congressmen don't seriously tackle the issue of hunger in deprived areas,.......................is a pity.

e. The charities .... I am a member of organise free meals for Christmas.

❷ Reliez les phrases à l'aide de relatifs.

I gave money to a man. He used the money to buy food.
→ *I gave money to a man who used it to buy food.*

a. The Red Cross is a charity. It distributes recycled food.
....
....

b. This is my sister. She is very cautious about not wasting anything. She brings the leftovers to her neighbours. They are always very thankful.
....
....
....

c. The Food bank is five minutes away from my home. It distributes food boxes.
....
....

d. I always bring 5 kilos of potatoes. It helps to feed a whole family.

....
....

e. I know these volunteers. They don't consume all their food. They recycle some food.

....
....
....

❸ Vous inaugurez dans votre ville un réfrigérateur communautaire qui permet aux gens de déposer la nourriture qu'ils ne consomment pas et à d'autres, dans le besoin, de se servir. Vous créez une affiche pour en avertir la population.

(a) Avez-vous de la nourriture que vous ne consommez pas ?

(b) Et vous ne savez pas à qui donner cette nourriture ?

(c) Ne jetez pas la nourriture qui peut être recyclée.

(d) Les personnes qui en ont besoin vous en seront reconnaissantes.

(e) Quiconque veut participer est bienvenu(e).

OUR COMMUNITY FRIDGE IS NOW OPEN!

(a)

(b)

(c)

(d)

(e)

DEPOSIT OR COLLECT FOOD, IT'S FREE!

Émettre des hypothèses plus ou moins probables, des souhaits et des regrets

Les subordonnées en *if*

bordas
Flash
PAGE
exercices
supplémentaires
interactifs

IN A WORD

Il existe plusieurs façons d'exprimer le regret.

- Hypothèse sur un avenir possible : *if* + **sujet** + **présent simple**, **sujet** + **modal** (*will, can, may...*) + **BV** : *If I speak to my voice-activated computer, it will answer me.*

- Hypothèse moins probable, voire impossible (irréel du présent) : *if* + **sujet** + **prétérit modal**, **sujet** + **modal** (*would, could...*) + **BV** : *If I were you, I would put wifi in all the rooms.*

- Hypothèse impossible (irréel du passé) : *if* + **sujet** + *past perfect*, **sujet** + **modal** (*would, could...*) + *have* + **participe passé** : *If I had wanted, I would have installed solar panels.*

- Regret : *if* + **sujet** + *past perfect*, **sujet** + **modal** (*would, could...*) + *have* + **participe passé** : *If I had bought a bicycle instead of a car, I would have saved money.*
Le regret s'exprime aussi avec *I wish* + *past perfect* **modal** : *I wish I had installed an electric car garage.*

- Le souhait s'exprime avec *I wish* + **prétérit modal** : *I wish my hybrid car were faster.*

⚠️ *Be* devient *were* à toutes les personnes au prétérit modal.

1 Entourez le verbe ou groupe verbal qui convient.

*If I had enough money, I **will install** / ⟨**would install**⟩ / **would have installed** the air conditioning in all the rooms.*

a. If my parents **buy** / **bought** / **had bought** a robot vacuum cleaner, my life would be easier.

b. If I have money, I **will equip** / **would equip** / **would have equipped** my house with the latest technology.

c. If our house **is** / **were** / **had been** more recent, we would not have had to insulate the walls.

d. If an architect came in, he **will ask** / **would ask** / **would have asked** to change the design.

e. If my light bulbs **are** / **were** / **had been** connected, I will command the light with my voice.

2 Mettez les verbes entre parenthèses aux temps qui conviennent.

I wish my sister (switch off) the light when she leaves her room. → I wish my sister switched off the light when she leaves her room.

a. If we don't change our old bulbs to new power-saving bulbs, our electricity bill (rise) ....

b. My father wishes he (can) .... control our central heater from a distance.

c. If Paula (have) .... a face-recognition house key, she would have got into her house much faster.

d. If I installed a presence detector, the light (switch on) .... the moment I approached the gate.

e. Tim wishes he (not / buy) .... an air conditioner because it consumes too much.

3 Dans le cadre d'un projet de classe, vous interviewez une architecte d'intérieur sur la maison du futur. Complétez le début de cette interview.

a. Good afternoon, I'm honored to interview one of the greatest architects about the house of the future.

Thank you for inviting me. I'm delighted to be here.

b. *(Vous demandez ce qu'elle inventerait si elle le pouvait pour créer une maison vraiment écologique.)*

....

Well, I think "smart walls" that keep and release heat would be a great invention and very eco-friendly.

c. *(Vous demandez en quoi ces murs seraient écologiques si on les inventait.)*

....
....

It's simple: the house wouldn't need a traditional heating system, so they would save a lot of energy.

d. *(Vous remarquez que si on avait tous de tels murs, on pourrait aider à sauver la planète.)*

That would be amazing! ....
....

Yes, we could, but for the moment it's just an idea that needs to be researched and developed.

e. *(Vous ajoutez que si on développe l'idée, elle pourra vraiment exister.)*

So, ...

I really think it can.

Rapporter des paroles au présent et au passé
Le discours indirect

• Pour passer du discours direct au discours indirect :
– si le verbe introducteur est **au présent**, il n'y a pas de changement de temps dans la subordonnée :
   *Paul **says** (that) you **have** to practise the drums more often.*
– si le verbe introducteur est **au prétérit**, dans la subordonnée :
présent → prétérit : *"I want to join the band."* → *Kate **declared** (that) she **wanted** to join the band.*
prétérit → *past perfect* : *"I wanted"* → *She said she **had wanted**.*
auxiliaires modaux : (**will**) et forme passée (**would**): *Steve **mentioned** (that) he **would** learn the piano.*
   (**can → could**) ; (**shall → should**) ; (**may → might**)

• Si la parole rapportée est une question, on peut utiliser **wonder whether** : *"Does Sam play the harp?"*
→ *Kevin **wondered whether** Sam played the harp.*

⚠ Comme en français, quand le verbe introducteur est au passé, les expressions de temps et de lieu changent :
today → *that day / the other day* ; *here* → *there.*
Parfois il faudra changer le pronom selon les personnes impliquées : *I* → *You*

---

1 **Transformez les phrases suivantes au discours indirect.**
   Do you know Purcell's King Arthur? (Paul wondered)
   → *Paul wondered whether I knew Purcell's King Arthur.*

a. "Is Carla playing the violin?" (My father asked)
....
....

b. "Kevin went to London to record a new album." (Mike said)
....
....

c. "You must find a new singer for our band." (The producer declared)
....
....

d. "Stella can buy her favourite band's newly released album." (My mother mentioned)
....
....

2 **Transformez les phrases suivantes au discours indirect.**
   Peter wondered: "can I come?" to the concert?
   → *Peter wondered whether he could come to the concert.*

a. My father was asking my brother: "Do you want to start?" playing the piano.
   My father was asking my brother ....
....

b. My producer asked me: "Why didn't you finish writing your album?
   My producer asked me ....
....

c. Kevin's brother declared: "I will never sing" on a stage again.
   Kevin's brother declared ....
....

d. The drummer said "I had to play for two hours before being allowed to have a break".

The drummer said ....
....

e. The group leader said: "I may not finish my European tour the way I planned it".

   The group leader said ....
....

3 **Votre professeure de chant vous a donné des conseils hier. Écrivez à vos parents ce qu'elle vous a dit.**

(a) "You must breathe in deeply before you start singing."
(b) "You can spare your voice."
(c) "You shall keep your throat and neck muscles relaxed even when you are singing high notes."
(d) "Don't clear your throat too often / clearing your throat is like slamming your vocal cords together."
(e) "Doing it too much can make you hoarse." (= *aphone*)
(f) "When you have to sing in public, think about using your microphone correctly."

Hi Dad, hi Mum!
Yesterday I had my first singing lesson with Mrs Jackson, she's a real professional. She gave me some tips to improve. For example, she said that (a) ....
.... She also mentioned that (b)
.....................by holding my breath.
She added that (c) ....
....
Surprisingly, she mentioned the fact that (d) ....
.... She explained that
....
....................., and she warned me that
(e) ....
Finally, she said that (f) ....
....
.....................to avoid straining my voice."
She's great!
                                    Mike

GRAMMAR

GRAMMAR

Relier deux propositions à l'aide d'un mot de liaison
La phrase complexe

 **IN A WORD** Les **mots de liaison**, qui relient deux propositions, servent à exprimer :

- la cause : ***since**, **as** + sujet + V, **because (of)**, **owing to**, **due to** + V-ing / GN* : *Unfortunately some people feel excluded from society **because of** their disability.*
- la conséquence : ***consequently**, **as a consequence**, **that's why**, **therefore***
- le but : ***(not) to**, **in order (not) to**, **so as (not) to** + BV, **so that** + sujet + V* : *My school is transforming the building entrance **(in order) to** make it accessible / **so that** it becomes accessible.*
- l'opposition et le contraste : ***contrary to**, **as opposed to**, **unlike** + GN, **whereas**, **while** + sujet + V*
- le paradoxe et la concession: ***although**, **even though**, **however**, **nevertheless**, **(and) yet***

① Remettez les éléments dans l'ordre.
to – prejudice – more and more information campaigns – are – fight – in schools – there – all sorts of – against. → *There are more and more information campaigns in schools to fight against all sorts of prejudice.*

a. equal – to consider – I – want you – to you – everyone

....

b. speaking groups – victims of prejudice – there – help – in my city – in order to – are

....
....

c. into my office – for making fun of him – Tim – will call – so that – he apologises – to Ralph – I

....
....

d. all its buildings – does – accessible – our city – to make – ? – really want

....
....

e. so as to – our classmates – a presentation – to their difficulties – will make – sensitise – John – about the elderly

....
....
....

f. parents – any discrimination – don't want – suffer from – to – their children

....

② Servez-vous des mots de liaison pour relier les phrases.
Being different can be positive. It can teach people to be tolerant. → *Being different can be positive as it can teach people to be tolerant.*
for V-ing – therefore – consequently – because of – due to

a. Michael is prejudiced against people who don't share his opinions / I need to talk to him.

....
....

b. In some countries people still don't have access to decent health care / politicians need to change the laws.

....
....
....

c. My brother wasn't accepted in that school / his disability.

....
....

d. Andrew will be appreciated / help to inform his fellow students about the issue.

....
....

e. Sheila was strongly criticised / her lack of understanding.

....

44

3 **Reformulez les phrases suivantes en changeant de mot de liaison.**

John finds it difficult to change schools whereas Liam thinks it's quite easy.
→ *Unlike John, who finds it difficult to change schools, Liam thinks it's quite easy.*

a. Most people don't often think about accessibility whereas Mary always leaves a remark if she visits a public place where there is an accessibility problem.

Contrary to ....

....

....

....

b. Contrary to Cynthia who doesn't know any sign language, Suzanne is fluent in sign language.

Cynthia doesn't know any sign language as opposed

to ....

c. In the past, people with disabilities were not protected by equality laws while today they are protected.

In the past, people with disabilities were not protected

by equality laws, contrary to ....

....

d. Sarah said they needed to organise an integration day whereas the other members of the school committee didn't think it was necessary.

Sarah said they needed to organise an integration

day, as opposed to ....

....

....

4 **Lors d'une discussion en classe avec votre assistante américaine, vous échangez sur la manière dont les États-Unis et la France mettent en place des choses pour faciliter la vie des personnes à mobilité réduite. Complétez ce début de conversation.**

a. "So, what do you think about the inclusion of people with disabilities?"

You: "France has still a lot to do in that field *(vous expliquez que tous les lieux ne sont pas accessibles)* ....
...."

b. "Really? What do you mean?"

You: "Well, we need to see what's happening elsewhere. *(Vous signalez que contrairement à la France, les trottoirs (= sidewalks) aux États-Unis sont souvent pratiques pour les gens en fauteuil roulant.)*
....
...."

c. "I see. And what about inside the buildings?"

You: "For example *(Vous répondez que les portes des bâtiments publics américains ont des capteurs (= sensors) pour donner accès aux personnes en fauteuil.)* ....
....
.... This is not always the case in France.

d. "Hmmm... Why do you think that is?"

You: *(Vous dites que malheureusement en raison d'un manque (= lack of) d'intérêt et d'argent, les pouvoirs publics (= public authorities) n'investissent pas assez)* "
....

.... to make the life of people with disabilities less difficult.

Répondre aux consignes de la compréhension de l'oral

bordas
Flash
PAGE

vidéo

◠ Observe and analyse

1 Associez chaque étape de guidage à l'explication donnée.

COMPRÉHENSION DE L'ORAL

En rendant compte, **en français**, du document, vous montrerez que vous avez identifié et compris :
– la nature ❶ et le thème principal ❷ du document ;
– la situation, les événements, les informations ❸ ;
– les personnes (ou personnages), leur fonction ou leur rôle ❹ et, le cas échéant, leurs points de vue ❺ et la tonalité (comique, ironique, lyrique, polémique, etc.) de leurs propos ❻ ;
– les éventuels éléments implicites ❼ du document ;
– le but et la fonction du document (relater, informer, convaincre, critiquer, dénoncer, etc.) ❽.

> Je lis toujours attentivement les consignes ! Les sujets n'auront pas systématiquement de guidage ou le guidage peut être légèrement différent.

> Je n'oublie pas d'analyser le titre et la source du document sonore avant l'écoute et je lis les noms propres de la source pour les repérer par la suite.

Une publicité sert à vendre, un journal à informer, une bande-annonce à communiquer sur le film qui va sortir, une campagne à dénoncer, etc. ....

Partir de la première écoute ou du premier visionnage pour essayer d'identifier le thème principal. ....

Bien identifier s'il s'agit d'une publicité, d'une bande-annonce, d'un documentaire, d'un reportage, d'une interview... ....

S'appuyer sur les indices sonores, les mots-clés, les mots répétés et les aides visuelles, s'il y en a, pour bien saisir les faits, les informations et les détails. ....

A-t-on l'avis d'une personne en particulier ? Est-ce objectif ou subjectif ? S'il s'agit d'une vidéo : y a-t-il une façon particulière de filmer qui révèle un point de vue ? ....

Identifier les personnes qu'on entend / voit ou celles qui sont évoquées, noter leur nom, si possible, leurs fonction, métier et opinions. Relever les noms et adjectifs qui se réfèrent à eux. ....

Certains éléments peuvent porter sur le sujet ou les personnes : les images, le ton, la musique, le bruit de fond peuvent suggérer quelque chose qui n'est pas dit explicitement. ....

S'appuyer sur le ton des personnages et, s'il s'agit d'une vidéo, sur les images. ....

🔺 Practise

2 Lisez le résumé suivant et précisez le contenu de chaque partie.

Il s'agit d'une vidéo de type documentaire. Le sujet principal est la situation des bagnards à l'époque où l'Australie était une colonie pénitentiaire.

Plusieurs spécialistes sont interviewés :

Une historienne évoque les conditions de transport, notamment pour les
5 femmes et les enfants. On essayait de séparer les enfants des autres détenus en leur réservant les ponts inférieurs. Malgré leur statut de prisonniers, les enfants bénéficiaient de cours pour parfaire leur éducation.

À leur arrivée en Tasmanie, les garçons étaient formés pour travailler et les filles souvent placées comme domestiques dans des familles. Un historien
10 explique qu'il existait de nombreuses usines pour femmes en Tasmanie et en Nouvelle-Galles du Sud. Ces usines correspondaient à la fois à un établissement pénitentiaire et à l'endroit où les femmes détenues étaient placées à leur descente du navire en attendant de savoir où on allait les envoyer.

Ce document à visée informative est peut-être issu d'un site internet consacré
15 à la mémoire des ancêtres de nombreux Australiens ou projeté dans un musée.

Introduction : ....

Développement : ....
....
....

Conclusion : ....

> 💡 Je vérifie toujours que j'ai bien évoqué tous les points importants que j'avais pris en note.

> 💡 Je vérifie que j'ai bien abordé tous les points exigés dans le guidage. S'il n'y a pas de guidage, je garde les questions types en tête, elles peuvent me servir de base pour mon compte-rendu.

> 💡 Je me relis : même si c'est la compréhension qui est évaluée, la qualité du français a son importance.

IN A WORD Qu'il y ait ou non des consignes de guidage, il faut **organiser ses idées** pour montrer de façon claire ce qu'on a compris. Par ailleurs, il n'est **pas nécessaire de suivre l'ordre des consignes ni l'ordre du document** audio ou vidéo : il n'y a pas de plan type.

Have a go BAC
ÉVALUATION 1 | ÉVALUATION 2 | ÉVALUATION 3

> **EXAM PREP • 100-103, 116-124**

STRATEGY

▶ **3 Écoutez le document suivant et rendez compte en français de ce que vous avez compris.**

VIDÉO
Titre du document: **Celebrating Black History Month: Cecil Williams**
Source: **PBS, February 6th, 2020**

Repérer des informations précises

Identifying stressed words

1 Écoutez l'enregistrement et complétez le tableau.

Number of voices = ...	Type of document = ...	Words remembered : ....
Tone = ...	Probable main theme = ...	....
....		....
....		....

2 Écoutez l'enregistrement et surlignez les mots accentués dans les phrases ci-dessous.

a. It's hard to believe today that women were denied the right to vote.

b. Society has become radically different from the past.

c. The economic, social and societal changes that have taken place make today's world unrecognisable compared to the 19ᵗʰ century.

> Pour comprendre un document audio, je m'attache à repérer les mots accentués et les intonations.

3 Réécoutez l'enregistrement et soulignez les types de mots qui sont accentués.

Nouns – verbs – prepositions – auxiliaries – adjectives – adverbs – articles – pronouns

4 Réécoutez l'enregistrement et soulignez les types de mots qui ne sont <u>pas</u> accentués, puis complétez *In a word*.

Nouns – verbs – prepositions – auxiliaries – adjectives – adverbs – articles – pronouns

> **IN A WORD**
>
> • Les **mots lexicaux** (noms, ... / .... et ....) sont les mots-clés d'une phrase et ils sont ☐ accentués / ☐ inaccentués.
>
> • Les **mots grammaticaux** (prépositions, ..., ... et ....) sont ☐ inaccentués / ☐ accentués. On peut comprendre la phrase même sans ces mots en devinant le sens global.

5 Écoutez l'enregistrement et entourez les mots que vous entendez.

sin / seen – 19 / 90 – lose / loose – law / low – think / thing – thing / sing – force / fourth – bone / born – 18 / 80 – great / create

> Je n'hésite pas à réécouter pour faire la différence entre deux mots qui semblent très similaires.

Recognising intonation

6 Lisez les phrases et entourez la flèche qui correspond à l'intonation, puis vérifiez en écoutant l'enregistrement.

a. Climate change is something that concerns us all. ↗ ↘ ↗↘

b. There's a conference about climate change next week and I was wondering if you'd like to.... ↗ ↘ ↗↘

c. Would you like me to come with you? ↗ ↘ ↗↘

d. What time does it start? ↗ ↘ ↗↘

7 Associez maintenant chaque type de phrase à son intonation.

> **IN A WORD**
>
> *Yes / No questions* (questions fermées) •
>
> *Wh-questions* (questions ouvertes) •   • ↗
>
> Affirmations •   • ↘
>
> Phrases incomplètes •

 **Practise**

8 **Construisez des phrases complètes à partir des mots proposés.**
Going cinema tonight – want come? call! ➜ *I'm going to the cinema tonight. Do you want to come? Call me if you do!*

a. Bus late – tell teacher please? Thanks!

....

b. singing club – starting – tomorrow – after school – 10 students coming

....

🎧 **9** **Écoutez l'enregistrement et notez les mots accentués.**

1	
2	
3	
4	

🎧 **10** **Écoutez l'enregistrement et entourez l'intonation puis indiquez le type de phrase dont il s'agit.**

	Intonation	Type de phrase
1	↗ – ↘ – ↗ ↘	
2	↗ – ↘ – ↗ ↘	
3	↗ – ↘ – ↗ ↘	
4	↗ – ↘ – ↗ ↘	

🎧 **11** **Écoutez l'enregistrement et entourez les mots que vous entendez.**
14 / 40 – tins / teens – arrested / arresting – saw / so – rang / wrong – please / police – brick / break – know / now – waste / ways

  **Have a go BAC** ÉVALUATION 1 ÉVALUATION 2 ÉVALUATION 3   ➤ **EXAM PREP** • 100-103, 116-124

🎧 **12** **Écoutez l'enregistrement et notez les mots-clés et les intonations que vous entendez.**

Youths break into disused factory

Key words	Intonations

STRATEGY

13 **À partir de vos notes, rédigez en français quelques lignes sur ce que vous avez compris sur feuille séparée.**

Anticiper, mettre en relation, synthétiser

bordas
Flash
PAGE
audios

◆ Observe and analyse

1 Lisez les titres des enregistrements et entourez les mots-clés.
Notez dans les cadres tous les mots qui vous viennent à l'esprit.

Je pars des mots-clés des titres pour élargir le champ lexical et imaginer les mots que je vais entendre.

1. Aid worker found not guilty of helping border-crossing migrants in Arizona .

3. Today's kids' health will be endangered by climate change .

2. Indian student excels in high-tech field.

2 Écoutez les enregistrements et reliez chaque audio à son titre (ci-dessus).   1 ....   2 ....   3 ....

3 Écoutez l'enregistrement et entourez le type de document auquel il correspond. Puis notez ce qui vous a aidé.
police series – comedy – debate – speech – advertisement – vintage radio show – interview

....

4 Notez quelques indices qui vous aideraient à identifier la tonalité de documents sonores que vous pourriez écouter.

Type of document	Clues
Police series	
Comedy	
Debate	
Advertisement	
Vintage radio show	
Interview	

5 Écoutez les enregistrements et devinez la fin des phrases. Entourez votre choix.

a. a sun lamp – the influence of alcohol – arrest

b. remain silent – call your mother – sing a song

c. friends and family – next guest – neighbours

d. disgusting – delicious – delighted

e. passed – went on holidays – failed

f. the UK – Ireland – the USA

g. rise – kneel down – turn around

Je m'appuie sur le contexte pour imaginer le sens des mots inconnus ou difficiles à entendre.

 **IN A WORD** On peut **anticiper un contenu** à partir d'un titre, d'un bruitage / fond sonore, du nombre de voix / du ton ou du début d'une phrase.

🔺 Practise

6 Anticipez le contenu du document sonore à partir de ce nouveau titre.

▶ | Titre du document | *Student Darnell Terry on how he manages money*

Source : **Dayton Youth Radio, NPR (National Public Radio), January 30ᵗʰ, 2020**

....

....

🎧 **7** Écoutez l'enregistrement pour vérifier. Identifiez le type de document, le nombre de locuteurs et le sujet. Notez dans le cadre ci-dessous les mots que vous retenez.

Type of document: .... **Number of speakers:** ....

Subject: ....

> 💡 J'écoute le document deux ou trois fois. À chaque écoute, je change de couleur pour prendre des notes.

8 Classez les mots retenus dans le tableau ci-dessous. Puis trouvez un titre pour chaque colonne.

9 Servez-vous du tableau pour synthétiser le document en quelques phrases en anglais ou en français.

....

....

....

....

> 🔊 **IN A WORD** Il est **inutile de comprendre chaque mot** pour comprendre et résumer un document sonore : en partant des **mots accentués / mots-clés** et en les classant par **thématique / champ lexical**, on peut reconstruire le sens et créer des liens.

STRATEGY

Have a go BAC

ÉVALUATION 1 ÉVALUATION 2 ÉVALUATION 3

▶ **EXAM PREP · 100-103, 116-124**

🎧 AUDIO

10 Restituez le contenu du document en français.

Titre du document: **News for teens by a teen: Olivia Seltzer**
Source: **NPR (National Public Radio), 08/09/2019**

Comprendre une vidéo ▸ 46, 48

bordas
Flash
PAGE

vidéos

🔴 Observe and analyse

1 Lisez le titre et notez les idées qui vous viennent à l'esprit et les mots que vous vous attendez à entendre.

*How **students feel** about new **school security** measures since the **Parkland shooting***

Source : **PBS (Public Broadcasting Service),** *News Hour,* **Feb 14, 2019**

IN A WORD

Comme pour un audio, le **titre** et la **source** permettent d'identifier des **éléments essentiels** (thématique, pays, noms propres, date, type de source...).

▶ 2 Regardez la vidéo une fois sans le son pour vous concentrer sur l'image : notez les mots qui vous viennent à l'esprit pour chacun des points suivants.

VIDÉO

Type of document / source: ....

People: ....

Places: ....

Time: ....

Theme: ....

Pour une vidéo, je pense aussi aux mouvements de caméra, au cadrage et au montage, notamment s'il s'agit d'un extrait de film ou d'une bande-annonce.

▶ 3 Regardez maintenant la vidéo en entier avec le son et vérifiez vos hypothèses. Entourez les mots ou idées que vous aviez bien anticipés en 1 et 2. Ajoutez quelques mots après ce premier visionnage.

....

....

▶ 4 Écoutez la vidéo une fois sans les images pour noter tous les mots accentués et répétés. Notez-les dans le cadre ci-dessous.

🔺 Practise

> Les images m'aident à comprendre et elles peuvent révéler ce qui est implicite (non dit).

🎧 **5** **Faites un dernier visionnage avec le son pour compléter les informations ci-dessus et créer des liens entre son et image** (expressions des visages / tons de la voix – images / commentaires – etc.). Puis classez les informations par thématiques dans le tableau ci-dessous en trouvant des intitulés à chaque rubrique.

places	...	...	...	...

IN A WORD
- L'**image** permet d'aider à **identifier** les personnes qui parlent, les expressions de leurs visages, le contexte, et donne de nombreuses informations, mais **peut aussi être trompeuse** : tout n'est pas présent à l'écran.
- Le **son** permet de bien **identifier** les mots accentués, répétés et le ton des interventions. Il est important de **faire un lien** entre le **son** et l'**image**.

6 **Organisez vos notes, en français ou en anglais, dans un plan structuré sur feuille séparée.**

Have a go BAC

ÉVALUATION 1   ÉVALUATION 2   ÉVALUATION 3

➤ **EXAM PREP · 100-103, 116-124**

▶️ **7** **Prenez des notes sur la vidéo en fonction des rubriques (title – picture – sounds) sur feuille séparée.**

VIDÉO
Titre du document: **Mimco X Ethical fashion initiative in Kenya 2018**
Source: **Clare Press recorded a podcast while in Kenya on Mimco X Ethical fashion initiative, August 2018**

8 **À partir de vos notes, faites la synthèse en français.**

STRATEGY

Répondre aux consignes de la compréhension de l'écrit

Observe and analyse

1 **Lisez ces consignes et soulignez les mots-clés qui vous semblent importants. Puis reliez les boîtes aux éléments que vous avez soulignés.**

Identifier le sujet principal n'est pas toujours possible à la première lecture. Si nécessaire, répondez d'abord aux autres questions. N'hésitez pas à lire le texte plusieurs fois.

Pour comprendre qui sont les personn(ag)es d'un texte (présent(e)s et mentionné(e)s), il faut chercher les noms propres, les pronoms, les références à des personnes et trouver les liens entre tous ces éléments.

Compréhension de l'écrit

Give an account **in English** and in your own words of text 1 and then of text 2.

In your account of text 1:

a- Identify:

- the main topic of the text;

- the people involved;

- their opinion on the topic.

b- Comment on the following paragraph and explain…

In your account of text 2:

a- Focus on the following three clues:

– I. …

– I. …

– I. …

b- Explain what they reveal about the narrator and why he is doing that.

After your accounts of texts 1 and 2, answer the following question:

Which text is more realistic? Justify.

On peut souligner de différentes couleurs les opinions en fonction des personnes pour identifier rapidement ce que chacun pense.

Certaines questions demandent à analyser un extrait du texte et à en reformuler le sens.

Certaines consignes vous invitent à observer des citations. Bien relire ce qui précède et suit ces citations permet de trouver les points communs et de comprendre le sens implicite à reformuler.

Certaines consignes concernent plusieurs textes. Ces questions demandent de porter un regard plus global sur les textes. Il est donc recommandé d'avoir répondu aux questions sur chaque texte au préalable.

2 **Lisez *In a word* et ajoutez vos idées personnelles sur la meilleure façon d'appréhender une évaluation de compréhension de l'écrit.**

....
....
....
....
....

IN A WORD

Lire les **consignes de compréhension de l'écrit avant** de **lire le texte** peut aider à connaître les attentes du jury. Elles ne doivent **pas** forcément être traitées **dans l'ordre**.
Appliquer des **stratégies de lecture classiques** (repérer les personnages, lieux, dates, champs lexicaux) est souvent **utile** et permet ensuite de revenir aux questions en ayant déjà bien compris le texte.

◠ Practise

3 **Reliez chaque consigne en anglais à ce qui est attendu.**

Comment ●   ● Je reformule dans mes propres mots.

Explain ●   ● Je cite le texte entre guillemets en indiquant
la ligne.

In my opinion ●   ● Je donne mon avis.

Justify by quoting ●   ● Je cible un élément dans le texte.

Focus on ●   ● Je réagis sur un point.

What can you say about ●   ● J'illustre en donnant un exemple du texte.

Give examples ●   ● Je trouve des informations sur les personnages,
les lieux…

4 **Lisez les consignes ci-dessous, soulignez les mots-clés puis entourez les compétences attendues pour chacune d'elles.**

Using all the documents…

…explain all the reasons why…   reformuler – synthétiser – développer – comparer

…describe and comment on the various points of view… reformuler – synthétiser – développer – comparer

…compare the past and the present…   reformuler – synthétiser – développer – comparer

…draw parallels with…   reformuler – synthétiser – développer – comparer

5 **Classez les expressions utiles pour répondre à des consignes de compréhension de l'écrit dans le tableau ci-dessous.**

> Je vérifie toujours que j'ai bien abordé tous les aspects présents dans les questions.

The main topic is… – The main characters are… – The story / scene is set in… – The article deals with… – What's striking is that…. – We can guess that… – The reason we know this is that…. – And I quote: "…". – When the narrator says (…) he / she implies that… – What is suggested is that… – Given the situation it seems likely / unlikely / inevitable that… – I can only agree with X when he states… – If I can rephrase that… – The main idea here is that… – The way I see it, … – In my opinion… – As far as I'm concerned… – It seems to me that… – I say that because… – This can be justified by the fact that…

> Je me relis : même si c'est la compréhension qui est évaluée, la clarté de la réponse est importante pour montrer que le texte est bien compris.

STRATEGY

Introduce / describe	Comment	Give your opinion

Quote / give examples	Explain	Justify

Comprendre un texte littéraire

Flash PAGE
PDF
DYS

🔴 Observe and analyse: global understanding

1 Lisez la source du texte et cochez ce que vous vous attendez à lire puis survolez le texte du regard et dites quels sont les éléments qui sont visuellement facilement identifiables.

I'd been in Cambridge a year when Steven arrived. He'd also come to Girton to read Economics. "Does it rain here often?" This was the first thing Steve said to me. Except he said "rhine," not rain, and I stared at him thinking, *What?* He was standing behind me in the lunch queue, a tall and skinny eighteen-year-old, with a wooden tray in his hand. He repeated his question in response to my blank
5 look, scarlet cheeked now. When I figured out what he'd said, I still thought, *What?* I gave some uninterested reply and turned to the curly-haired boy who was with him – Kevin, he told me his name was – hoping for a more inspiring chat. Steve later told me he thought, you arrogant cow.

The two of them quickly became the comics in our group. They regaled us with wildly exaggerated impersonations of characters from their local neighbourhoods, savouring the knowing that in
10 Cambridge they would not be maimed for this, as they would be back home.

Steve and Kevin relied on each other to navigate Cambridge, an untried terrain for these two working-class boys, Steve from East London and Kevin from Basildon in Essex. So that at the sherry reception to meet the Mistress of the college, Steve nudged Kevin as he told her, "Me and my friend we want to…" but too late, she corrected him and said "You mean, my friend and I."
15 In those days, Steve wore a green bomber jacket, Doc Martens boots, and a West Ham football scarf. This look of urban toughness was at once defeated because his grandmother had knitted STEPHEN across his scarf, as you would for a five-year-old.

So they'd act the thief who stole the neighbour's TV and displayed it in his own living room – even though the neighbour was a friend who often popped over for a chat (and probably to watch
20 *Crimewatch UK*, who knows). Or "hard men" who strutted the street saying, "You looking a' me or chewing a brick?" and were affronted if you looked them in the eye. And those with ambitions to make it big in the world of crime – wannabe bank robbers and bare-knuckle fighters who lived by the code of not "grassing up" friend or foe to the law.

Sonali Deraniyagala, *Wave. A Memoir of Life after the Tsunami*, 2013

☐ un texte récent   ☐ un texte ancien   ☐ un texte littéraire   ☐ un texte journalistique

Éléments visuellement identifiables

....

2 Lisez le texte et notez tous les mots comprenant une majuscule (en dehors des majuscules de début de phrase) et classez-les en trois rubriques, puis donnez un titre à chaque rubrique.

3 Notez en français ce que vous pensez être le sujet principal et le contexte du texte.

....
....
....

> Si je ne connais pas le contexte, les personnages, le pays, je peux imaginer et vérifier lors de la prochaine lecture.

Observe and analyse: detailed understanding

4 Relisez le premier paragraphe reproduit ci-dessous puis lisez les boîtes autour du texte pour découvrir les principales stratégies de comprehension.

5 Utilisez différentes couleurs pour surligner des exemples de chaque stratégie dans le texte.

PLACES
Explicite : observez les noms propres ou références à des lieux pour répondre à la question 'where?'.
Cambridge = GB / probably Cambridge University

PEOPLE
Explicite : observez les pronoms / noms / références aux personnes pour répondre à la question 'who?'
I = narrator

TIME
Explicite : observez les références à des moments / dates / saisons / durées pour répondre à la question 'when?'
a year = time the narrator spent at Cambridge

IMPLICIT MEANING
Implicite : réfléchissez aux implications par associations d'idées.
he speaks differently = he might be from another place / country or from a different social background

MORE DETAILS
Explicite : trouvez des informations supplémentaires sur les personnes (description, activités, sentiments...).
A tall skinny eighteen-year-old = the characters are probably all young / students

STRATEGY

DYS

> I'd been in Cambridge a year when Steven arrived. He'd also come to Girton to read Economics.
>
> "Does it rain here often?" This was the first thing Steve said to me. Except he said "rhine," not rain, and I stared at him thinking,
> 5 *What?* He was standing behind me in the lunch queue, a tall and skinny eighteen-year-old, with a wooden tray in his hand. He repeated his question in response to my blank look, scarlet cheeked now. When I figured out what he'd said, I still thought, *What?* I gave some uninterested reply and turned to the curly-
> 10 haired boy who was with him – Kevin, he told me his name was – hoping for a more inspiring chat. Steve later told me he thought, you arrogant cow.
>
> **Sonali Deraniyagala,** *Wave. A Memoir of Life after the Tsunami,* 2013

OTHER CLUES
Implicite : servez-vous des éléments mis en valeur (italique, répétitions, ponctuation...) pour comprendre.
What?
= the narrator feels shocked / surprised / speechless / maybe because he / she is not used to social / geographical differences

Practise: detailed understanding

6 Servez-vous des repérages pour répondre à la question sur le premier paragraphe. *Who and what is the passage about?*

People :

Number	Names	Age / Physical description	Other information
present :	....	....	....
mentioned:	....	....	....
....	....	....	....

> Si la réponse n'est pas dans le texte, j'émets des hypothèses à partir de ce que j'ai compris.

Place: ....

Time: ....

7 Complétez le tableau : *What can you guess about the characters' social background?*

Information in the text p. 57	Characters implied	Implicit meaning / probable feelings
"Does it rain here often?" (l. 3)	....	....
he said "rhine," not rain (l. 4)	....	....
I stared at him thinking, *What?* (l. 4-5) / (...) I still thought, *What?* (l. 8-9)	....	....
scarlet cheeked (l. 7-8)	....	....
uninterested reply (l. 9)	....	....
hoping for a more inspiring chat (l. 11)	....	....
Steve later told me (l. 11)	....	....
you arrogant cow (l. 12)	....	....

8 Résumez ce que vous avez compris du premier paragraphe dans vos propres mots en anglais.

This passage is about ... .

....

....

....

9 **Appliquez les stratégies pour comprendre la suite du texte : complétez les deux tableaux.**

The two of them quickly became the comics in our group. They regaled us with wildly exaggerated impersonations of characters from their local neighbourhoods, savouring the knowing that in Cambridge they would not be maimed for this, as they would be back home.

5 Steve and Kevin relied on each other to navigate Cambridge, an untried terrain for these two working-class boys, Steve from East London and Kevin from Basildon in Essex. So that at the sherry reception to meet the Mistress of the college, Steve nudged Kevin as he told her, "Me and my friend we want to…" but too late, she corrected him and said "You mean, my friend and I."

10 In those days, Steve wore a green bomber jacket, Doc Martens boots, and a West Ham football scarf. This look of urban toughness was at once defeated because his grandmother had knitted STEPHEN across his scarf, as you would for a five-year-old.

Sonali Deraniyagala, *Wave. A Memoir of Life after the Tsunami*, 2013

People: present: .... mentioned:	Names	Physical description	Other information
Place:			
Time:			

Information in the text p. 59	Characters implied	Implicit meaning / probable feelings
the comics in our group (l. 1)		
untried terrain (l. 5)		
Me and my friend (l. 8)		
she corrected him (l. 8)		
look of urban toughness (l. 11)		
grandmother had knitted STEPHEN (l. 12)		

STRATEGY

Comprendre un texte littéraire (suite)

bordas
Flash
PAGE
PDF
DYS

Observe and analyse: guessing unknown words

10 Lisez le dernier paragraphe une fois et relevez l'information essentielle dans le texte.

DYS

So they'd act the thief who stole the neighbour's TV and displayed it in his own living room – even though the neighbour was a friend who often <u>popped over</u> for a chat (and probably to watch *Crimewatch UK*, who knows). Or "hard men" who <u>strutted</u> the street saying, "You looking a' me or <u>chewing a brick</u>?" and were affronted if you looked them in the eye. And those with ambitions to
5 <u>make it big</u> in the world of crime – <u>wannabe</u> bank robbers and <u>bare-knuckle</u> fighters who lived by the code of not "<u>grassing up</u>" friend or <u>foe</u> to the law.

Sonali Deraniyagala, *Wave. A Memoir of Life after the Tsunami*, 2013

People: ....

Place: ....

11 Expliquez en quelques lignes de quoi parle ce passage.

....

....

....

12 Concentrez-vous sur les mots soulignés et complétez le tableau sans utiliser de dictionnaire.

Word or expression	Grammatical category	Probable meaning	How I guessed
popped over (l. 2)			
strutted (l. 3)			
chewing a brick (l. 4)			
make it big (l. 5)			
wannabe (l. 5)			
bare-knuckle (l. 5)			
grassing up (l. 6)			
foe (l. 6)			

IN A WORD
Pour comprendre un texte littéraire, il faut se concentrer d'abord sur ce qu'on comprend immédiatement. Ensuite, on cherche les **informations principales** (*people / places / time*). Il ne faut **s'attarder** sur les **mots inconnus** que s'ils sont importants pour comprendre le **sens** du texte. On peut **s'appuyer** sur la nature du mot, le contexte immédiat (ce qu'il y a avant / après) et **sur ce qu'on a compris** pour essayer de deviner le sens.

Si je ne comprends pas le sens d'un mot sans dictionnaire, je reformule le sens de la phrase en m'appuyant sur ce que j'ai compris.

Have a go BAC
ÉVALUATION 1 | ÉVALUATION 2 | ÉVALUATION 3

➤ EXAM PREP • 104-127

13 Utilisez le repérage réalisé pour répondre aux questions type bac suivantes.

a. After reading the whole text (▶ 56), what can you say about the two main characters and their origins / backgrounds?

b. Focus on the following clues:
– "The two of them quickly became the comics in our group." (line 8, paragraph 2)
– "She corrected him and said 'You mean, my friend and I.'" (line 14, paragraph 3)
– "In those days, Steve wore…" (line 15, paragraph 4)
What do they reveal about Steve and Kevin compared with other people?

c. Explain how other people see them.

d. What can you say about the kind of life the people in Kevin and Steve's hometowns had?

STRATEGY

Comprendre un texte journalistique

STRATEGY

🔻 Observe and analyse

① **Avant de lire le texte, observez les éléments périphériques (= titre, sous-titre, source) puis complétez.**

Time: .... Country: ....

Topic: ....

> Les titres et les sous-titres permettent d'émettre des hypothèses sur le sujet, le contexte (l'élément déclencheur de l'article) et la question principale.

Not too shabby: what will it take to make secondhand clothes mainstream?

Through mending, lending and <u>adopting</u> a fast-fashion ethos, secondhand <u>shopping</u> is slowly shaking off its <u>stigma</u> in Australia.

When it comes to fashion, we didn't always have a fetish for newness.

Just ask <u>historian</u> Robyn Annear. The way she tells it in her new book, *Nothing New: A History of Second-Hand*, the <u>Industrial</u>
5 <u>Revolution</u> changed everything. Before then most of <u>humanity</u> wore secondhand. (…)

> Dans un article, il y a souvent une idée par paragraphe : **le premier mot** (ainsi que les mots-clés) peuvent aider à comprendre le sens global du paragraphe.

Once factory-made clothes came on the market, "people were <u>encouraged</u> to buy new **stuff** and to want new stuff and to afford new stuff," Annear says. The <u>quality</u> wasn't always amazing, but
10 new clothes were marketed as respectable, hygienic, even patriotic. Of course, they were also on <u>budget</u>, and on-trend.

Because the new stuff looked so new, it made the old stuff look *old*. So secondhand became a charity case, fit only for those who had no other choice. In the <u>popular</u> western <u>imagination</u>, old
15 clothes <u>symbolised</u> <u>poverty</u> or sloppiness or neglect. (…)

But now that <u>stereotype</u> has grown a bit old too. One recent study from the US online **thrifting** <u>platform</u> thredUP <u>predicted</u> that America's secondhand apparel market will double in the five years from 2018 (US\$24bn[1]) to 2023 (US\$51bn). (…)
20 **So what** makes secondhand work for 21st-century eyes used to novelty and mass <u>production</u>? The thredUP model is **geared towards** an Instagram-friendly, outfit of the day **churn**, where customers update their looks fast. Ownership doesn't last forever. The secondhand outfit is purchased, worn, enjoyed, uploaded to
25 socials, and then <u>recycled</u> back into the sales network. (…)

> Le dernier paragraphe est souvent un condensé de l'article et résume les conclusions.

So how do we make secondhand work for us now? We shop smart, we mend and <u>embellish</u> and, if needed, we lie. The <u>cult</u> of newness hasn't **unravelled** just yet. But its secondhand challenger isn't looking too **shabby** either.

Jo Walker, theguardian.com, November 19th, 2019

1. bn = billion

> Les toutes premières lignes d'un article exposent souvent la situation / le contexte.

> La source de l'article donne des indications sur la date, l'année et le type de presse.

DYS

2 Lisez le texte et les encarts. Reliez chaque partie du texte à son contenu.

"When" → "neglect" (l. 1-15) ●   ● secondhand clothes today

"But now" → "US$51 bn" (l. 16-19) ●   ● secondhand and new clothes are both part of how we shop today

"So" → "network" (l. 20-25) ●   ● secondhand clothes in the past

"So how" → end (l. 26-29) ●   ● why secondhand clothes are popular again

3 Observez les mots soulignés et dites pourquoi vous les comprenez facilement.

Ce sont des mots... ....

4 Observez les mots surlignés en vert et entourez le sens probable de chacun
en vous servant du contexte.

Unknown word	Probable meaning		Unknown word	Probable meaning
stuff	rubbish – clothes – things		churn	misconception – problem – variations
thrifting	expensive – money-saving – controversial		unravel	reduce – increase – discover
geared towards	intended for – not destined to – beautiful		(not too) shabby	(not too) old – (not too) pretty – (not too) bad

> Je m'appuie sur ce qui est facile (les chiffres, les majuscules, les mots répétés, les mots transparents).

 **IN A WORD** Pour comprendre un **texte journalistique**, on commence par le **paratexte** : titre, sous-titre, source. On poursuit en s'appuyant sur le **premier** et le **dernier paragraphes** et sur les chiffres, les dates, les mots avec des majuscules.

 **Have a go** BAC ÉVALUATION 1 ÉVALUATION 2 ÉVALUATION 3   ➤ EXAM PREP • 104-127

5 Utilisez les stratégies apprises pour vous aider à comprendre l'intégralité du texte et répondre aux questions type bac suivantes.

a. After reading the text what can you say about:
– the main topic of the text?

....
....

– the situation in the past?

....
....

– the situation today?

....
....

b. Explain the effect of Instagram and social media on the fashion choices people make today.

....
....
....
....

STRATEGY

Comprendre deux textes de nature différente

bordas
Flash
PAGE

PDF
DYS

◖ Observe and analyse

1 Observez les paratextes et complétez les boîtes avec le mot approprié : « littéraire » ou « journalistique ».
Puis lisez chacun des textes et vérifiez que les informations se confirment.

▶ **Text A**

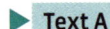

DYS

Fortune suddenly smiled upon Jo, and dropped a good luck penny in her path. Not a golden penny, exactly, but I doubt if half a million would have given more real happiness then did the little sum that
5 came to her in this wise[1].

Every few weeks she would shut herself up in her room, put on her scribbling[2] suit, and 'fall into a vortex'[3], as she expressed it, writing away at her novel with all her heart and soul, for till that was
10 finished she could find no peace. (…)

Well, it was printed, and she got three hundred dollars for it, likewise plenty of praise and blame, both so much greater than she expected that she was thrown into a state of bewilderment[4] from which it
15 took her some time to recover.

"You said, Mother, that criticism would help me. But how can it, when it's so contradictory that I don't know whether I've written a promising book or broken all the ten commandments?" cried poor
20 Jo.

(…)

Her family and friends administered comfort and commendation[5] liberally. Yet it was a hard time for sensitive, high-spirited Jo, who meant so well and
25 had apparently done so ill. But it did her good, for those whose opinion had real value gave her the criticism which is an author's best education, and when the first soreness[6] was over, she could laugh at her poor little book, yet believe in it still, and feel
30 herself the wiser and stronger for the buffeting[7] she had received.

"Not being a genius, like Keats[8], it won't kill me," she said stoutly, "and I've got the joke on my side, after all, for the parts that were taken straight out
35 of real life are denounced as impossible and absurd, and the scenes that I made up out of my own silly head are pronounced 'charmingly natural, tender, and true'. So I'll comfort myself with that, and when I'm ready, I'll up again and take another."

Louisa May Alcott, *Little Women*, 1868

1. in this wise (exp.) = in this way – 2. scribble (v.) = write quickly
3. vortex (n.): *tourbillon* – 4. bewilderment (n.): *confusion*
5. commendation (n.) = praise – 6. soreness (n.): *douleur*
7. buffeting (n.) = beating
8. John Keats is an English Romantic poet (1795-1821)

La source :
Dans un texte
.... ,
le type de source et la date sont souvent importants pour donner une indication sur le contexte.

Dans un texte
.... ,
l'auteur peut être connu et la date donner une indication sur le style d'écrit, le siècle et le contexte général.

Le titre :
Pour un texte
.... ,
le titre donne une indication précise sur le contenu.

Pour un extrait de texte
.... ,
le titre de l'œuvre n'indique pas toujours ce dont va parler le passage.

Le temps utilisé :
Le texte
....
est le plus souvent au présent.

Le texte
....
est souvent au prétérit, temps de la narration.

▶ **Text B**

Sister Act: How Little Women has Come of Age on the Big Screen

Greta Gerwig's new big-screen adaptation of *Little Women*, the sixth about the March sisters to be made so far, starts with a scene taken from the middle of Louisa May Alcott's second volume. Almost all the others have begun with the girls' childhood, but in Gerwig's film, we first meet an
5 adult Jo March in the New York offices of the *Weekly Volcano*, where she hopes to place a story – thus setting it up as a film about writing. Along with all the things we expect from this story (coming of age, sibling[1] relations, the challenge of being good), the film is about the relationship of fiction with life, and the challenges and the rewards of writing as a
10 job. The parallels between Jo and her creator, Alcott, are also drawn out

by Gerwig, and this adult Jo co-exists throughout the film with the child Jo, who is learning how to write, how to
15 be a woman and, often, how similar these processes can be.

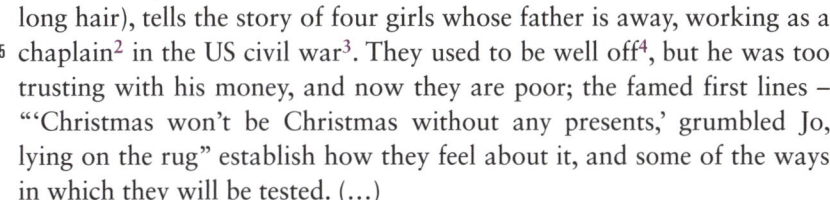

Published in the late 1860s, *Little Women*, for those for whom mentions of Meg, Jo,
20 Beth and Amy do not instantly evoke scenes known since childhood (a book-burning, the shearing of a head of

long hair), tells the story of four girls whose father is away, working as a
25 chaplain[2] in the US civil war[3]. They used to be well off[4], but he was too trusting with his money, and now they are poor; the famed first lines – "'Christmas won't be Christmas without any presents,' grumbled Jo, lying on the rug" establish how they feel about it, and some of the ways in which they will be tested. (…)

30 We may these days (…) be surrounded by books containing extraordinary girls – Lyra, Hermione, Katniss – but it is striking that they are exceptions, and often alone; groups of girls in, say, the *Gossip Girl* books are toxic and destructive. *Little Women* is about "a world of women, of value in and of itself". It is also, Gerwig has said, "one of the few books about
35 childhood that isn't about escape. There is bravery, but it's a hero's journey contained inside the home." And one whose male characters are peripheral. In the first volume Jo, furious that Meg is thinking of getting married, thus breaking up the cosy family, rages that "buds will be roses, and kittens cats – more's the pity". In Gerwig's film Meg replies to a
40 similar outburst[5] with: "Just because my dreams are different from yours doesn't mean they're not important." Perhaps the truly radical thing is that Alcott tried to make space and time for all of them.

Alder Eldermariam, theguardian.com, December 7ᵗʰ, 2019

1. sibling (n.) = brother or sister – 2. chaplain (n.) = military clergyman –
3. US civil war = 1861-1865 – 4. well off (adj.) = rich – 5. outburst (n.): *explosion*

IN A WORD
Un coup d'œil rapide suffit souvent pour repérer la **différence** entre un **texte journalistique** et un **texte littéraire**.
– Présence / absence d'un **titre**.
– **Source** : récente, plus datée, comportant un titre de roman ou non.
– **Temps** : temps de la narration (prétérit) ou présent, etc.
– **Style** : factuel, journalistique ou littéraire.

Comprendre deux textes de nature différente (suite)

bordas
Flash PAGE
PDF DYS

Practise

2 Lisez les textes à nouveau et reportez dans les tableaux toutes les références aux personnes, lieux et éléments temporels. Puis soulignez en bas de chaque colonne ce qui est le plus fréquent pour chaque texte.

Novel

People	Places	Time
personnages fictifs – personnes réelles	mentionnés explicitement – non mentionnés explicitement	marqueurs temporels – dates précises – présent – prétérit

> Pour me repérer facilement, je surligne les informations dans les textes en utilisant trois couleurs différentes.

Article

People	Places	Time
personnages fictifs – personnes réelles	mentionnés explicitement – non mentionnés explicitement	marqueurs temporels – dates précises – présent – prétérit

> Comme les informations ne sont pas toujours données explicitement, je cherche des indices.

3 Lisez les extraits suivants puis cochez dans le tableau (page de droite) à quel texte correspond chaque caractéristique. Citez ensuite un ou deux exemple(s) tiré(s) du texte que vous avez coché(s) pour justifier votre réponse.

DYS 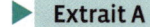 **Extrait A**

Fortune suddenly smiled upon Jo, and dropped a good luck penny in her path. Not a golden penny, exactly, but I doubt if half a million would have given more real happiness then did the little sum that came to her in this wise.

Every few weeks she would shut herself up in her room, put on her scribbling suit, and 'fall into a vortex', as she expressed it, writing away at her novel with all her heart and soul, for till that was finished she could find no peace. (…)

Well, it was printed, and she got three hundred dollars for it, likewise plenty of praise and blame, both so much greater than she expected that she was thrown into a state of bewilderment from which it took her some time to recover.

> Pour comprendre un texte littéraire, je peux commencer par identifier les personnages, les lieux ou les références temporelles : ces stratégies m'aideront à situer l'essentiel de l'explicite. Ensuite, je relis pour trouver plus de détails et comprendre l'implicite.

DYS ▶ Extrait B

We may these days (…) be surrounded by books containing extraordinary girls – Lyra, Hermione, Katniss – but it is striking that they are exceptions, and often alone; groups of girls in, say, the *Gossip Girl* books are toxic and destructive. *Little Women* is about "a world of women, of value in and of itself". It is also, Gerwig has said, "one of the few books about childhood that isn't about escape. There is bravery, but it's a hero's journey contained inside the home." And one whose male characters are peripheral.

> Dans un article, je commence toujours par regarder le paratexte, le début et la fin du texte puis le début de chaque paragraphe pour me faire une idée du sujet.

	Text A literary	Text B journalistic	Examples
Character's personality / feelings			
Comments / opinions			
Implicit elements			
Multiple examples			
Steps of a story			
Description / facts			
Hypotheses			
Literary devices (metaphores)			

STRATEGY

IN A WORD

– Un **texte journalistique** est destiné à être lu rapidement. Il comporte souvent une **idée** par **paragraphe**, est écrit dans un **style direct** avec souvent **peu d'implicite**.

– L'extrait de **texte littéraire** est souvent tiré d'un roman plus long, il faut donc souvent **imaginer** ou **reconstituer** les **sentiments** des personnages et certains **éléments de l'histoire**.

Répondre aux consignes de l'expression écrite

Observe and analyse

1 Associez chaque sujet d'expression écrite à un type d'écrit (= *genre*). Soulignez, dans le sujet, les indices qui vous ont mené sur la voie.

Sujets d'expression écrite			Genre
Write an email to your best friend to tell him / her about your holiday in London.	●	●	*Courriel*
Imagine a conversation between a graffiti artist and a policeman.	●	●	*Discours*
Explain what you think are the strong and weak points of going to university.	●	●	*Texte argumentatif*
Write an article for your school magazine about the advantages and drawbacks of taking a gap year.	●	●	*Journal intime*
Write a post on your blog to tell your English-speaking followers about an event you are organising.	●	●	*Article*
You have just been voted student of the year and you are invited to give a speech.	●	●	*Éditorial / article d'opinion*
Your family has just moved to Scotland. Write about your journey and arrival in your diary.	●	●	*Post de blog ou de forum*
You have decided to write an article for your school magazine to speak out against child slavery.	●	●	*Dialogue*

… I would never want to travel in space. It's a waste of time and money.

Which one do you agree more with? Why? ● ● *Lettre*

… Travelling in space would be an amazing once in a lifetime experience.

Write to your town hall to talk about the need for a youth club in your town. ● ● *S'exprimer à partir d'une citation*

IN A WORD Pour analyser une consigne d'expression écrite : **partir des mots-clés** pour clarifier le contexte (situation, rôle, etc.) et **identifier le style exigé** par le type d'écrit : courriel, article, entrée pour un blog, journal intime, discours, texte argumentatif, opinion sur une citation, opinion personnelle, etc.

Si, le jour de l'évaluation, je tombe sur un type d'écrit que je n'ai jamais rencontré : pas de panique, le bon sens m'aidera à réfléchir aux caractéristiques de ce type d'écrit.

🔴 Practise

2 **Reliez chaque type d'écrit à ses caractéristiques en vous aidant si nécessaire des pages *Strategy* correspondantes.** ▶ 70-83

e-mail ●   ● donner son point de vue dans un écrit organisé qui vise à convaincre

speech ●   ● adapter son niveau de langue à la personne à laquelle on s'adresse et penser aux formules de politesse

essay ●   ● adapter le niveau de langue à la situation et aux personnages et utiliser la ponctuation appropriée

diary ●   ● adopter un style neutre et factuel et respecter les codes du genre

article ●   ● écrire dans un style formel en suivant un plan bien établi au préalable

opinion piece / editorial ●   ● utiliser des stratégies pour capter l'attention de son auditoire

quotation-based expression ●   ● partir d'une citation pour donner son opinion en justifiant ou expliquant son point du vue

dialogue ●   ● utiliser un style informel, personnel, intime

> Je prends le temps de bien réfléchir à la spécificité de chaque écrit avant de commencer.

3 **Lisez les sujets suivants, appliquez les conseils ci-dessus pour noter dans la colonne de droite vos idées de structure, de contenu et de style.**

> Je pense à l'axe auquel se rattache le sujet pour m'aider à trouver des idées de contenu.

Sujet	Genre	Contents
Comment on these words by artist Francis Bacon: "Truth is so hard to tell, it sometimes needs fiction to make it plausible."		

Sujet	Genre	Contents
You are given the choice to listen to one of these podcasts. Which one do you choose and why? – It's Baton Rouge: Out to lunch. Food history in Louisiana's capital. – Canadian music podcast: in-depth interviews with artists, industry experts & more. – CBS Sports Eye on college basketball.		

Sujet	Genre	Contents
Should everyone spend at least one year abroad in his / her life? Explain why or why not.		

Sujet	Genre	Contents
Write a post about your favourite TV series for your class blog. Explain what it is about and give the reasons why you like it.		

STRATEGY

Exprimer une opinion

◗ Observe and analyse

1 Soulignez les mots-clés dans ce sujet.

> Do you think that art can change the way people think? Give an example to illustrate your point of view.

2 Pour chaque mot-clé, notez les idées qui vous viennent à l'esprit.

....

....

....

3 Lisez la copie ci-dessous et retrouvez le plan que l'élève a suivi en complétant les cases.

....

....

....

> **DYS**
>
> Art, whatever its form, can have a strong impact on people's emotions.
>
> Personally, I cry every time I watch my favourite TV series. However, can art actually change the way people think?
>
> I'm not convinced that art can really change people's minds about anything. In my opinion, it can only inform you, or reinforce what you already think. As far as I'm concerned, we are essentially attracted to the art that reflects our thoughts, although I'm prepared to admit that it may depend on the art and on the person.
>
> To conclude, it seems to me that art is a unique and personal experience, appreciated by most people, but we are who we are and we think what we think, regardless of art.

> 💡 Je me méfie des faux amis. *Actually* se traduit par vraiment / en fait. Actuellement se traduit par *currently / nowadays*.

4 Soulignez l'exemple donné qui illustre le point de vue.

5 Surlignez ce qui résume l'opinion dans le dernier paragraphe.

6 Identifiez la stratégie utilisée pour faire la transition entre l'introduction et la partie principale.

....

....

◗ Practise

7 Listez les mots et expressions qu'on peut utiliser pour exprimer une opinion, puis complétez avec les synonymes que vous connaissez.

Words and expressions in the text	Synonyms I know

8 Trouvez les mots et expressions utilisés pour lier des idées dans une phrase (▶83) puis complétez avec d'autres mots que vous connaissez.

Words and expressions in the text	Synonyms I know

9 Concentrez-vous sur les verbes et entourez la forme verbale utilisée le plus souvent. Expliquez pourquoi.

simple present – présent *be* + *V-ing* – past simple – past perfect simple – present perfect simple

....

....

IN A WORD

Pour **exprimer son opinion à l'écrit**, il faut :

• **Analyser le sujet** : relever les mots-clés – identifier la nature du sujet et la tâche à accomplir

• **Réfléchir** : noter les mots qui viennent à l'esprit

• **Organiser ses idées** : faire un plan structuré - lister les expressions utiles

• **Rédiger** : Rédiger son introduction – développer chaque partie – soigner ses transitions – illustrer avec des exemples – rédiger une conclusion – se relire

Have a go BAC ＞＞＞

ÉVALUATION 1 | ÉVALUATION 2 | ÉVALUATION 3

> **EXAM PREP • 104-127**

10 Utilisez ce que vous avez appris pour donner votre opinion sur le sujet suivant (120 mots au moins).

Do you think that art should be obligatory for all high school pupils?

a. Entourez les mots-clés dans le sujet. Notez toutes les idées qui vous viennent à l'esprit.

Je fais une carte mentale au brouillon.

b. Faites un plan.

c. Notez les mots et expressions à utiliser pour exprimer une opinion.

d. Listez les mots et expressions que vous pouvez utiliser pour lier vos idées.

e. Choisissez le temps que vous allez utiliser pour exprimer votre opinion.

f. Écrivez votre texte.

Je n'oublie pas de me relire !

STRATEGY

Écrire un courriel

Observe and analyse

1 Lisez les deux courriels puis remettez dans le bon ordre les conseils suivants pour écrire un courriel.

 DYS

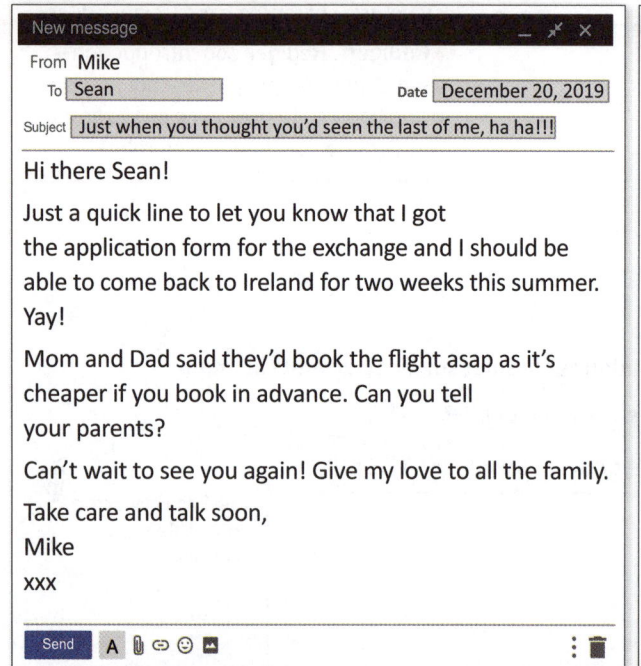

New message — ⤢ ×

From **Mike**
To **Sean**   Date **December 20, 2019**
Subject **Just when you thought you'd seen the last of me, ha ha!!!**

Hi there Sean!

Just a quick line to let you know that I got
the application form for the exchange and I should be
able to come back to Ireland for two weeks this summer.
Yay!

Mom and Dad said they'd book the flight asap as it's
cheaper if you book in advance. Can you tell
your parents?

Can't wait to see you again! Give my love to all the family.

Take care and talk soon,
Mike
xxx

Send A 🔗 😊 🖼   ⋮ 🗑

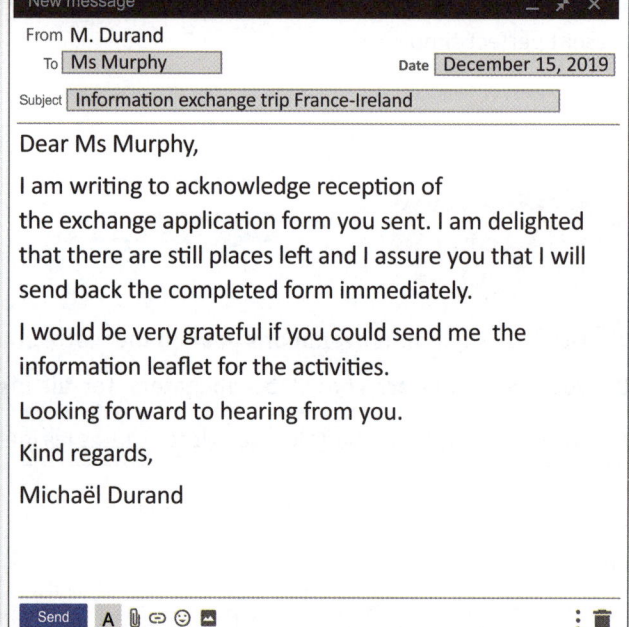

New message — ⤢ ×

From **M. Durand**
To **Ms Murphy**   Date **December 15, 2019**
Subject **Information exchange trip France-Ireland**

Dear Ms Murphy,

I am writing to acknowledge reception of
the exchange application form you sent. I am delighted
that there are still places left and I assure you that I will
send back the completed form immediately.

I would be very grateful if you could send me the
information leaflet for the activities.

Looking forward to hearing from you.

Kind regards,

Michaël Durand

Send A 🔗 😊 🖼   ⋮ 🗑

Rédiger des paragraphes courts, avec une idée par paragraphe et en commençant avec les informations les plus importantes – Débuter par une formule de politesse – Conclure par une formule de politesse – Écrire un objet précis et bref

1.	
2.	
3.	
4.	

2 Soulignez dans les deux courriels les formules et les expressions et classez-les en séparant l'anglais informel de l'anglais formel.

	Informal English	Formal English
A. Greetings (to open)		
B. Expressions confirming reception		
C. Expressions to ask for something		
D. Greetings (to close)		

🔺 Practise

3 **Classez les formules de politesse suivantes dans le tableau. Ajoutez d'autres expressions que vous connaissez.**

Dear Sir / Madam – Hey! – To whom it may concern – See you soon – Take care for now – Best regards – Do you want to…? – All the best – Cheerio – Hi! – Let me know what… – Kind regards – Talk soon – Would you mind telling me…? – Sorry about… – Yours faithfully – If it is not too much trouble, I would like to know… – Before I go… – Hello there! – I'd like to present my apologies for… – Yours sincerely – One more thing…

	Greetings (to open)	Expressions to ask for something	Greetings (to close)
Informal English			
Formal English			

📢 **IN A WORD** Un **courriel** doit être **concis** : il faut inclure le **but principal** dans le **premier paragraphe** puis rédiger des **paragraphes courts** (un point principal par paragraphe). On doit penser à **adapter son niveau de langue** à la personne à qui l'on s'adresse et à conclure par une **formule de politesse**.

Have a go BAC

ÉVALUATION 1 | ÉVALUATION 2 | ÉVALUATION 3

➤ **EXAM PREP · 104-127**

4 **Vous traiterez en anglais et en 120 mots au moins le sujet suivant : You have a British correspondent who has just gone home after spending two weeks with you. Write a mail to him / her about the experience and asking about your visit to stay with him / her which is planned for next month.**

New message _ ⤢ ✕

From	
To	
Subject	

Send   A 📎 🔗 😊 🖼   ⋮ 🗑

STRATEGY

Écrire un discours

bordas
Flash
PAGE

PDF
DYS

Observe and analyse

1 Lisez le texte et identifiez le sujet principal et le public. Qu'en déduisez-vous concernant la personne qui parle ?

....

....

2 Parcourez le texte à nouveau et soulignez les répétitions, la question et la citation. Dites à quoi elles peuvent servir.

....

3 Concentrez-vous sur la manière dont la révélation de l'identité de Stephen Hawking crée du suspense. Notez à côté de chaque paragraphe ce que vous apprenez de plus sur lui.

DYS

> Je structure mon discours avec des transitions claires et marque des pauses. Je pense à m'entraîner à voix haute !

Teachers, fellow students,

When we, the students, were asked to agree on a name for the new science lab, we quickly realised that many great women and men would deserve to be our choice. How could we possibly make this decision? However, after a long discussion, one person stood out. One man, born and raised here in the UK, who was confronted with terrible challenges throughout his life and who faced those challenges with courage, strength and humour.

This scientist never gave up. Despite every obstacle, he never stopped searching to understand the universe. And thanks to his work, we understand the universe better. Perhaps more importantly, this brilliant scientist has inspired us to keep learning, to keep fighting for knowledge.

As he once said: *"Look up at the stars and not down at your feet. Try to make sense of what you see, and wonder about what makes the universe exist. Be curious."*

Stephen Hawking. A scientist, a genius, a legend, an inspiration. Though he is no longer of this world, he has left us with a light that will never go out.

IN A WORD Avant d'écrire un discours, il faut **définir en amont le sujet** et **savoir à qui on s'adresse**. Le discours étant **voué à être prononcé**, il faut, dès l'écriture, trouver le **rythme adapté** en utilisant des **phrases courtes**, des **répétitions** judicieuses et des mots-clés pertinents. Différentes techniques permettent d'attirer l'attention de son auditoire comme la question rhétorique, l'anecdote, le suspense et l'émotion.

Have a go BAC

ÉVALUATION 1   ÉVALUATION 2   ÉVALUATION 3

➤ **EXAM PREP • 104-127**

4 Vous traiterez en anglais et en 120 mots au moins le sujet suivant : You have been chosen to make a speech to announce the name to be given to the new school gymnasium and the reasons for the choice.

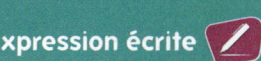

Écrire un dialogue

🔴 Observe and analyse

1 Observez la ponctuation utilisée au début du dialogue puis insérez la ponctuation manquante à partir de la ligne neuf, paragraphe cinq.

"We are so in trouble!" whispered Sarah, as she and Samia walked down the corridor towards Mrs Byrne's office that Monday morning.

"Do you think she will understand if we explain it to her?" asked Samia hopefully.

5 "Don't count on it," Sarah replied in a low voice, "you know how strict she can be, she'll probably scream 'Excuses, girls, nothing but excuses!', as she always does. Still," she added, "it's worth a try."

They knocked on the head teacher's door.

Come in Good morning girls please be seated Mrs Byrne's invitation
10 was polite but serious

Mrs Byrne please let us explain We thought that Mr John would appreciate our joke as he *loves* Shakespeare pleaded Sarah

Samia interjected Yes it's true He's *always* quoting Hamlet in literature class Alas poor Yorick while holding an imaginary skull in the air

15 Oh, indeed he does admitted Mrs Byrne However Miss Jones was less happy with the disappearance of the skull from her science lab You'll need to bring her back the skull and apologise immediately Although Mrs Byrne's tone was firm her eyes were twinkling

IN A WORD

Écrire un dialogue implique un **choix de situation et de personnages** (personnalité, relation entre les personnages, raisons de la discussion, issue probable). Le **ton** et le **registre** doivent être **adaptés** à la situation et le cadre précisé. Il est recommandé de **varier les verbes** introducteurs et d'**enrichir le dialogue** d'adverbes pour qualifier les actions et les personnages. La **ponctuation** doit être soignée.

2 Complétez le tableau.

Introduction verbs	Characters (how they are linked)	Action (where, what, when, why)

3 Que remarquez-vous par rapport aux formes verbales ? Entourez la bonne réponse.

Les paroles des personnages sont au présent / au prétérit alors que le reste du texte est au présent / au prétérit

ÉVALUATION 1 ÉVALUATION 2 ÉVALUATION 3

➤ EXAM PREP • 104-127

4 Sur feuille séparée, vous traiterez en anglais et en 120 mots au moins le sujet suivant :
Write the dialogue between Samia, Sarah and Miss Jones using the following guidelines:

– *The girls bring back the skull to the lab;*
– *Miss Jones asks for an explanation;*
– *The girls explain and apologise;*
– *Miss Jones gives them a punishment and accepts their apology.*

STRATEGY

Rédiger un article

🔴 Observe and analyse

❶ Observez la structure de l'article puis complétez les étiquettes autour à l'aide des informations ci-dessous.

date – conclusion – middle paragraphs – subtitle – opening paragraph – title

---

→ Where's our water?

Water Thieves Steal 80,000 Gallons in Australia making *Mad Max*-Style Fiction Become Reality ←

→ 15/12/19 8:00AM

Thieves stole about 80,000 gallons of water in a region of Australia that's suffering from one of the worst droughts in the history of the country. And with record-breaking heat it feels like Australia is living in the future. That future, unfortunately, looks a lot like *Mad Max*. ←

Police in New South Wales report that a farmer in the small town of Evans Plain had about 80,000 gallons of water stolen from his property. The theft from two enormous storage tanks could have happened at any time between December 9 and December 15, according to authorities.

It's becoming more and more common to see thieves targeting water storage facilities, as climate change continues to devastate → Australia as it heads into summer. Just a couple of weeks ago, thieves stole about 6,600 gallons of water, enough to fill about six or seven fire trucks, according to local authorities.

→ All in all, it all feels like something out of a sci-fi dystopia, where water wars are fought to survive. More and more Australians are wondering how long it will take the Prime Minister to get serious about this issue.

adapted from earther.gizmodo.com

---

❷ Lisez le titre et le sous-titre et déduisez le sujet principal du texte.

....

....

❸ Lisez le texte et reliez chaque paragraphe à sa description.

Paragraph	Description
....	Summary / commentary about the event and / or the questions it raises
....	More general information about the theme / other similar events
....	Essential information about the main event
....	Additional information about the main event

❹ Focalisez-vous sur le titre et le premier paragraphe.
Retrouvez les informations correspondant aux questions suivantes.

Who? ....

What? ....

Where? ....

When? ....

Why? ....

5 Concentrez-vous sur les deuxième et troisième paragraphes.
Notez les sources d'information et les verbes / expressions utilisés pour les évoquer.

Sources d'information : ....

Verbes/expressions: ....

6 Lisez le dernier paragraphe et relevez une expression utilisée pour résumer un contenu.
Ajoutez d'autres expressions que vous connaissez.

....

7 Relisez tout le texte :

– notez les formes verbales les plus fréquentes

....

– entourez les mots correspondant à son style et son ton

informatif – informel – objectif – subjectif – formel – polémique – humoristique

IN A WORD

Pour écrire un article, il faut :
– trouver un **titre** et un **sous-titre** qui donnent une idée claire du sujet et incitent à la lecture ;
– organiser des **paragraphes**, en commençant par l'essentiel pour aller vers les détails,
les informations plus générales et les commentaires plus personnels ;
– choisir le **ton** et le **style** ;
– utiliser un **langage formel**.

Have a go BAC

ÉVALUATION 1 ÉVALUATION 2 ÉVALUATION 3   ➤ **EXAM PREP · 104-127**

8 Vous traiterez en anglais et en 120 mots au moins le sujet suivant : Your school has decided to introduce a ban on plastic bottles. Write an article for the school magazine using the information below.

water fountains will be installed — students can buy a reusable cup for 1 euro — teachers and students voted in favour of the measure — the aim is to help the environment — other schools may follow the example

Think of an attractive title and subtitle.

Organise your article into clearly defined paragraphs, beginning with the essential information.
Find a conclusion that is thought-provoking and engages the reader.

Je veille à la qualité de mon anglais et j'apporte une touche personnelle pour rendre mon article plus attrayant.

STRATEGY

Écrire un texte argumentatif

Observe and analyse

① **Lisez le texte et associez les catégories avec les extraits du texte.**

DYS

Sujet : Should 16-year-olds be given the right to vote ?

The right to vote, whatever the country, was a long battle that lasted many years. Indeed, for a long time it was reserved to the privileged few. Today we have come a long way. However, in a rapidly-changing world where decisions made today may impact future generations, shouldn't young people be able to vote from the age of 16 instead of 18?

5   On the one hand, some people argue that 16 is far too young to vote. They maintain that in order to know who to vote for you need to be mature enough to understand what is going on in the world and to analyse political messages. Though such arguments are perfectly logical in many respects, they do not take into account the fact that young people today are educated and, what's more, have much easier access to information than in the past.

10   On the other hand, a growing number of people believe that young people should be allowed to weigh in on urgent questions that will impact their future. After all, we are the ones who will live with the consequences of any bad decisions. Furthermore, young people can be very active and bring a fresh approach to issues, as we have seen with Greta Thunberg, for instance.

For all of these reasons, I am convinced that allowing young people of 16 to vote would enhance
15   rather than damage democracy.

main question ●	● would enhance rather than damage democracy
historical context ●	● Greta Thunberg
context today ●	● should 16 year-olds be given the right to vote?
arguments against the main question ●	● important decisions being made in an evolving world
arguments in favour of the main question ●	● much too young, need to be mature to understand and analyse
example ●	● young people are educated, have easier access to information; will impact their future, have to live with the consequences of any bad decisions, can be very active and bring a fresh approach
conclusion ●	● voting severely restricted / a long fight

② **Retrouvez le plan suivi en numérotant.**

[......] arguments for   [......] arguments against and comments on them   [......] personal opinion   [......] introduction

③ **Lisez à nouveau le texte et soulignez les expressions / mots de liaison correspondant aux rubriques du tableau, puis classez-les selon leur fonction.**

Introduce an example / justification	Add information	Contrast

Concede	Express a goal	Introduce an opinion	Sum up

IN A WORD Pour écrire un **texte argumentatif**, il faut : bien **cerner le sujet**, rassembler ses idées au brouillon et **formuler une opinion**, puis noter des **exemples** pour la **justifier**. Réfléchir ensuite aux **autres opinions possibles** et trouver des **arguments** pour les **contrer**. Organiser ses idées en faisant un plan puis rédiger en utilisant des expressions et mots de liaison appropriés pour faire des **transitions** et **nuancer** son propos.

Je me relis, je vérifie l'intelligibilité et la cohérence de mon texte et je corrige les erreurs de langue.

🔴 Practise

Je souligne les mots-clés du sujet et je mobilise le lexique adapté.

4 Utilisez ce que vous avez appris pour écrire un texte argumentatif sur le sujet suivant. Complétez le tableau puis élaborez un plan (= *outline*).

Sujet : Should public transport be free?

Ideas	
Words and expressions	
My opinion	
Arguments against and my reactions	

Your outline : ....

5 Rédigez votre texte (100-120 mots).

Have a go
BAC

ÉVALUATION 1 ÉVALUATION 2 ÉVALUATION 3

➤ **EXAM PREP • 104-127**

6 Vous traiterez en anglais et en 120 mots au moins le sujet suivant :
Is equality just an impossible dream?

Écrire un texte narratif

Observe and analyse

1 I was born in a little village just a few miles from Glasgow. My first memories of home (…)

2 Detective Brown knew as soon as she laid eyes on Micky Murphy that he would be trouble. He was wearing a loose-fitting jacket to hide his gun (…)

3 Mary woke up suddenly with her heart pounding in her chest. The rain was lashing against the window. Was it a dream or had she heard the sound of glass breaking downstairs?

4 I watched Sun-5 as he parked his instant travel tube outside the compound and waited for the automatic sensors to recognise him and open the main door. What had brought him back again?

1 Lisez les textes et complétez le tableau à l'aide de votre lecture et des informations ci-dessous.

Genre : science-fiction – policier – thriller – biographie

Type de narration : 1re personne – 3e personne – narrateur interne (fait partie de l'histoire) – narrateur externe – narrateur lit / ne lit pas dans les pensées des personnages

	Genre	Narrative style	Characters
1			
2			
3			
4			

2 Soulignez les formes verbales dans les textes et notez ci-dessous les plus fréquentes.

IN A WORD Écrire un **texte narratif**, c'est **choisir un genre** et décider des **personnages**, du **lieu** et du **contexte** ; adopter un **style de narration** et inventer une **intrigue**. Il faut structurer son texte et inclure des éléments pour garder l'intérêt de ses lecteurs. Enfin, il faut utiliser les formes verbales appropriées et ne pas oublier de se relire.

Practise

> Je peux m'inspirer d'un style ou un genre que j'aime bien et j'ose me risquer à les imiter.

3 Vous allez écrire un texte narratif : entourez vos idées favorites dans le tableau ci-dessous.

Genre:	Characters:	Place:	Time:	Event:	Narrator:
detective – thriller – science fiction – autobiography – romance	suspect – villain – victim – hero – heroine – devious – honest – traumatised	town – countryside – seaside resort – castle – manor house – school	now – 19th century – holidays – childhood	events leading up to the main event – main event (= climax) – following events	part of the story – outside of the story= first person / third person narrative

4 Placez les événements de votre histoire sur une frise chronologique.

....

....

....

....

....

[frise chronologique avec flèche et points]

....

....

....

5 Choisissez votre point de départ sur votre frise et écrivez vos premières phrases en essayant de capter l'attention de vos lecteurs (une question, une exclamation, une émotion forte...).

....

....

....

....

6 Maintenant écrivez votre histoire !

....

....

....

....

....

....

....

....

....

....

....

STRATEGY

Have a go
>> BAC   ÉVALUATION 1 ÉVALUATION 2 ÉVALUATION 3

➤ **EXAM PREP • 104-127**

7 Vous traiterez en anglais et en 120 mots au moins le sujet suivant :
You are a secret graffiti artist and every night you go out to paint a new work of art that you feel has a message. Imagine a night when something happens...

> spray paint – colourful – neglected – bring beauty – controversial – conviction – deserted – grey – miserable – bring hope – police car – siren – flee – whistle – handcuffs – warning – unexpected – friendship – complicity

....

....

....

....

....

....

....

Écrire un journal intime

bordas
Flash
PAGE

PDF
DYS

🔴 Observe and analyse

1 Lisez et relevez les expressions utilisées pour commencer et terminer la page de ce journal intime.

Pour commencer : ....

Pour terminer : ....

DYS

> *Monday, 5ᵗʰ April*
>
> Dear diary,
>
> What a day I've had! As you know there was a school trip to the Science Museum today and I really wasn't bothered about going. I thought it'd be dead boring,
> 5 a total yawn-fest, but in fact I was completely blown away by it. There were literally tonnes of things to do and see. I didn't realise you could get to do real experiments. Really awesome! Of course Nate acted the idiot as usual and nearly had us all thrown out because
> 10 of his behaviour. Mr Mason really told him off and made him stay right beside him for the rest of the visit, like a 2-year-old. It was so hilarious we couldn't stop laughing at him, and the more we laughed, the more Nate sulked. Ha, it served him right.
>
> 15 Anyway, a fantastic day, I'm so glad I decided to go in the end. I think I need to learn a lesson from this: don't judge a book by its cover (unless it's Nate, ha ha, what you see is what you get with him: an IDIOT!! Even if he's incredibly good-looking, in fact drop-dead
> 20 gorgeous... STOP!)
>
> Time for bed, YAWN!! Back tomorrow!

2 Soulignez les mots qui expriment des sentiments et des opinions.

3 À qui fait référence *"you"* (ligne 1)? Entourez la bonne réponse.

le narrateur – le lecteur – le journal

4 Entourez les formes verbales les plus fréquemment utilisées.

le prétérit – le *past perfect* –

les temps du présent – modal + BV

5 Entourez les mots qui décrivent le mieux le style.

formel – informel – personnel –

polémique – objectif

> **IN A WORD**
> Quand on écrit dans un journal intime, on **s'adresse** souvent **au journal comme si** c'était une **personne** qui nous est **chère**. On lui **raconte sa journée** : les événements clés, ses sentiments, ses espoirs et ses peurs. Il faut commencer et terminer en utilisant une **formule de politesse** simple et informelle. Les temps utilisés sont essentiellement le **présent** et le **prétérit**.

Have a go BAC

ÉVALUATION 1   ÉVALUATION 2   ÉVALUATION 3

> **EXAM PREP • 104-127**

6 Vous traiterez en anglais et en 120 mots au moins le sujet suivant : You have had a really memorable day at school... Write an entry in your diary. Ideas: *back to school after the summer break – important exams / exam results – last day at school – arrival of some exchange student*.

Enchaîner les idées

bordas
Flash
PAGE
PDF
DYS

🔴 Observe and analyse

1 Lisez le texte ci-dessous et soulignez les mots qui servent à relier les idées.

> To begin with people can feel very differently about the British royal family, depending on their background, their political views or their character. On the one hand, some love the glamour, the entertainment factor, or the traditional side. On the other (hand), it has been argued that they are a waste of taxpayers' money. For a start, some of the family members expect to have a private life while holding a public position. Secondly, they are born into wealth instead of earning it through hard work, unlike many ordinary citizens. Last but not least, we have proof all over the world that societies can function well without a royal family. Despite the arguments against their existence, as long as they earn a living I can accept being in a monarchy. I would say to conclude that unless there's a revolution I don't see them disappearing any time soon.

2 Recopiez les mots que vous avez soulignés dans le tableau ci-dessous selon leur fonction.
Ajoutez d'autres mots si vous en connaissez.

Organise ideas	
Express a condition	
Oppose ideas	
Speak about simultaneous events	
Present a paradox	

IN A WORD Pour **enrichir** et **structurer** son expression, il faut avoir **recours aux mots** et **expressions appropriés**. Certains de ces mots et expressions exigent une structure spécifique. ▶98

STRATEGY

🔴 Practise

3 Réécrivez le texte ci-dessous en ajoutant des mots et expressions permettant de relier les idées et en faisant les modifications nécessaires.

> It would be a good thing to ban cars in all centre towns. Some people would disagree. I think it would be really positive for the environment. I believe there would be fewer accidents. I am sure there would be less noise pollution. Some people need cars. They have disability issues. Banning cars could work. Public transport would need to be cheap. It would need to be easily accessible.

J'analyse bien le sens des phrases afin de pouvoir les relier avec des mots et des expressions appropriées.

STRATEGY

Parler en continu

🔴 Observe and analyse

1 Adopter la bonne attitude. Cochez la case lorsque la posture et l'attitude de la personne sont appropriées pour une présentation orale.

IN A WORD

Lorsqu'on s'exprime devant un **examinateur**, il faut **soigner sa posture** : se tenir droit(e), la tête haute, sans croiser les bras, et regarder son interlocuteur dans les yeux.

2 Savoir enchaîner des idées. Le script ci-dessous est une transcription du début de l'oral d'un candidat à partir d'une image. Réécrivez-le et enrichissez-le en piochant dans les expressions de la liste. Retrouvez les informations correspondant aux questions suivantes :

what we can see here is – which – so we can guess that – if you look closely you can see – what's more – to whom – it's clear to me that – indeed – in my opinion – what I think is that – furthermore – therefore – that's why

The photo is of a truck. It is open at the back. Inside we can see some fruit and vegetables. On the side of the truck is written "From our garden to your plate!" Some young people are talking to an elderly couple. They are handing them a basket with fruit and vegetables in it. The young people are wearing old clothes and muddy boots. They must have a garden where they grow produce to sell. It must be a start-up business. This illustrates the theme of Private space and public space. The young people are using their private space for a business idea.

....
....
....
....
....
....
....
....

ÉVALUATION 1   ÉVALUATION 2   **ÉVALUATION 3**

➤ **EXAM PREP • 116-127**

3 Choisissez parmi les documents A et B celui qui illustre le mieux, à votre sens, l'axe *Espace privé et espace public*. Vous disposez de 10 minutes de préparation. Puis présentez et expliquez votre choix en parlant pendant cinq minutes.

> **Gap-fillers:** how can I put it – actually – you know – I mean – you know what I mean – let me explain – let me clarify – Well, what I'm trying to say is

DOCUMENT A

Companies such as WeWork provide co-working office space where people can work, whether it's because they don't want to rent an office for their start-up or small business, for example, or because they work remotely and don't want to work from their home. People can have access to many services and equipment a traditional office has to offer, without having to deal with its inconveniences. The co-working concept has been growing and is expected to continue to do so over the next few years.

DOCUMENT B

"Women are responsible for two-thirds of the work done worldwide, yet earn only 10 percent of the total income and own 1 percent of the property. So, are we equals? Until the answer is yes, we must never stop asking."

Daniel Craig, British actor

STRATEGY

Réagir aux questions de l'examinateur

bordas Flash PAGE
audio

Observe and analyse

1 Lisez la citation proposée pour l'axe 8 *Territoire et mémoire*. Lisez des exemples de questions que pourrait poser l'examinateur et cherchez les liens avec l'axe (▸20). Soulignez les mots les plus importants dans les questions.

"Ceremonies are important. But our gratitude has to be more than visits to the troops, and once-a-year Memorial Day ceremonies. We honor the dead best by treating the living well."

Jennifer M. Granholm,
Canadian-American politician, lawyer, educator, author, and political commentator

☐ *Do you think that ceremonies are important to commemorate people and events?*

☐ *What traces of the past are noticeable in English-speaking countries like the USA, the UK, Australia and so on?*

☐ *Can you think of any examples of signs of the past that you can still see today in English-speaking countries?*

☐ *What can we learn from the past? Link your answer to an English-speaking country.*

☐ *Do you feel old buildings should be restored or should we make way for new architectural ideas?*

☐ *Can you talk about borders between any English-speaking countries? (England / Scotland – Northern Ireland / Ireland – the USA / Canada…)*

2 Cochez les questions qui étaient prévisibles selon vous, puis essayez de répondre à haute voix et sans notes à quelques questions (▸84). Écoutez des exemples de productions d'élèves.

Je m'enregistre et je réécoute mon enregistrement en analysant mes points forts et les points à améliorer.

Je peux aussi m'entraîner avec un camarade pour m'améliorer.

IN A WORD Devant l'examinateur, il faudra savoir réagir en **montrant ses connaissances des problématiques des axes** au programme. Si on connaît bien les problématiques de chaque axe, on peut **anticiper les questions**. Il faut **s'entraîner à répondre à haute voix** et sans préparation pour améliorer sa capacité à réagir spontanément.

Have a go

BAC

ÉVALUATION 1   ÉVALUATION 2   **ÉVALUATION 3**

▸ **EXAM PREP · 116-127**

3 Vous avez choisi l'axe *Citoyenneté et mondes virtuels* et décidé d'en parler à partir de cette citation.

Après votre présentation, vous allez échanger avec l'examinateur pendant cinq minutes. Voici des questions qu'il pourrait vous poser. Vous pouvez vous enregistrer et vous réécouter.

"In the cyber world, bullies have a wall to hide behind so they say things that they probably wouldn't say otherwise."

Nina Dobrev, Bulgarian-Canadian actress

Should Internet control be tighter?

How can cyberbullying be dealt with?

Citizenship and virtual worlds

What responsibility comes with freedom of expression?

As virtual citizens, what are our rights and responsibilities?

What are some basic rules that should be respected when posting on a forum?

What are the strong and weak points of social networks?

Améliorer sa prestation orale

Observe and analyse

🎧 **1** Une élève a parlé de l'axe *Art et Pouvoir* à partir de la citation ci-dessous.
Écoutez ses deux prestations et notez vos premières impressions sur feuille séparée.

> *Phil believed strongly that one could change events, or change people's perception, through a well-crafted song.*
>
> **Michael Schumacher,**
> *There But For Fortune: The Life of Phil Ochs,* 1996

2 Comparez les extraits de deux prestations à partir de leurs scripts et notez les points à améliorer :
richesse lexicale – mots de liaison / expressions pour donner son opinion / parler de ses sentiments – lien avec l'axe – fluidité

First try	Second try
"I don't know Phil Ochs, but maybe he's a singer? Because it says the word 'song' in the quotation. Maybe he wanted to change events and change people's perceptions with his songs. That's like Art and power. Art can be a power. (…) But only if the art is good, like a well-crafted song. But good art can change people's perception. I listen to music and I listen to the words and sometimes I think it's important and I want to change or I want to think differently about life, people, something. Phil Ochs maybe did that."	*"Although I don't actually know Phil Ochs, I can guess from the quotation that he must have been a singer who wrote songs to influence people. By all accounts his beliefs were quite strong, as he was a strong believer that a well-written song could impact real life. It's interesting that he specifies that this is only true of good quality songs. I don't know, maybe that's true, but it cannot be denied that such an opinion is subjective. The way I see things, who can define what a well-crafted song is? When studying Art and power this year, we came across some striking examples of art trying to have an influence on people and events or hoping to make people think. (…) On a personal level, as a music-lover myself, I do feel that some lyrics can have an impact on me and on the way I see people, my life and so on. To come back to the quotation, I suppose we can wonder if that's precisely what Phil Ochs did, proving that art can indeed be powerful."*

....

....

....

Practise

3 Choisissez un axe que vous avez travaillé en classe et listez les mots qui vous viennent à l'esprit.

> *Je cherche dans un dictionnaire bilingue les mots qui me semblent importants mais que je ne connais pas en anglais.*

4 Réfléchissez sans rien noter à la manière dont vous parleriez de cet axe à l'oral.
Ensuite, essayez d'en parler pendant une minute en vous enregistrant et en utilisant les mots que vous avez listés.

> *En cas de doute, je me sers d'un dictionnaire en ligne pour vérifier la prononciation des mots importants (wordreference.com).*

5 Réécoutez-vous. Remarquez-vous des erreurs, des répétitions ?
Vous pouvez recommencer si vous n'êtes pas satisfait(e) de votre enregistrement.

> *Je me construis un stock d'expressions et d'amorces de phrases que j'essaie d'utiliser quand je m'entraîne.*
> ▶ 98

 **IN A WORD** Pour améliorer la qualité de l'expression, il faut **s'entraîner à développer ses idées à haute voix**, avec des **phrases claires** et grammaticalement **correctes**, en **variant** les **choix lexicaux** ; et à relier ces phrases avec des **mots de liaison**.

STRATEGY

Créer des liens : de la compréhension de l'oral au compte-rendu en français

⬤ Observe and analyse

① Prenez connaissance du titre de l'audio et de sa source et notez ce que vous évoque chaque mot-clé.

[   ]   [   ]   [   ]

[   ]   *Navajo Indians going to college: a changing tradition –* Source: NPR (National Public Radio), "Weekend Edition Sunday", 18 February, 2018   [   ]

🎧 **② Écoutez l'audio trois fois et prenez des notes en anglais et/ou en français.**

....
....
....
....
....
....

> 💡 Je prends en note les mots et les idées que j'entends et ce que je devine.

⬤ Practise

③ Réorganisez vos notes en tenant compte des éléments donnés dans le guidage. ▶ 46-47

Nature, thème et but du document : ....
....

Situation / événements / informations : ....
....

Personnes : ....
....
....
....

> 💡 Je rassemble et j'ordonne les éléments pour avoir un compte-rendu cohérent.

> **IN A WORD** Rendre compte d'un document en français n'est pas traduire : il s'agit de **reformuler en réorganisant**, comme si on souhaitait expliquer à quelqu'un qui n'a pas entendu l'audio ce qu'on a compris.

Have a go BAC

ÉVALUATION 1   ÉVALUATION 2   ÉVALUATION 3

> **EXAM PREP • 100-103, 116-127**

④ Vous rendrez compte en français de ce que vous avez compris du document.

....
....
....
....
....
....
....
....

Créer des liens : de la compréhension de l'écrit à l'expression écrite

⬤ Observe and analyse

1 Lisez ce texte extrait de *Not too shabby...* (▶ 62). Lisez ensuite le sujet d'expression écrite qui lui a été associé et soulignez dans le texte les arguments qui pourraient vous être utiles pour y répondre.

> In the popular western imagination, old clothes symbolised poverty or sloppiness or neglect. (…)
> So what makes secondhand work for 21st-century eyes used to novelty and mass production? The thredUP model is geared towards an Instagram-friendly, outfit of the day churn, where customers update their looks fast. Ownership doesn't last forever. The secondhand outfit is purchased, worn,
> 5 enjoyed, uploaded to socials, and then recycled back into the sales network.
>   Likewise, the rise of Instagram resellers, (…) bring some of that shiny newness to the act of shopping for secondhand threads.
>
> **Jo Walker**, theguardian.com, November 19th, 2019

On a blog, you read three reactions from people who have just read the article *Not too shabby...*
Who do you most agree with? Why?

B. I used to think that second hand clothes were only for people who couldn't afford new clothes, but now I realise it's getting more and more trendy and I'm starting to buy some!

A. Secondhand clothes? No way! I could never wear something that has already been worn by someone I don't even know!

C. I have always been in favour of secondhand clothes: why should we manufacture new clothes that contribute to polluting the environment when we can recycle?

Je m'inspire du texte mais je ne recopie pas : je reformule dans mes propres termes.

STRATEGY

⬤ Practise

2 Choisissez l'une des citations et notez vos idées en mêlant celles inspirées par le texte et vos idées personnelles.

....

....

....

....

....

....

 **IN A WORD** Les expressions écrites sont liées à la thématique du dossier : il est possible de **réutiliser certains arguments du texte** si on veille à les **mêler** à d'autres **arguments plus personnels**.

 **Have a go BAC** `ÉVALUATION 1` `ÉVALUATION 2` `ÉVALUATION 3`   ▶ **EXAM PREP · 104-127**

3 Entraînez-vous à répondre par écrit au sujet suivant à partir du même texte en appliquant les conseils ci-dessus sur feuille séparée (120 mots ou plus).

To what extent has the Internet changed the way people see secondhand clothes? Give examples.

Créer des liens : synthétiser des informations à partir de documents divers

🔴 Observe and analyse

Ce dossier comprend : une vidéo (document 1), un texte journalistique (document 2) et un texte littéraire (document 3).

▶ **DOCUMENT 1**

Titre du document : *Could we Live Forever? Transhumanists Give their Opinion*

▶ **1** Regardez le document **1** plusieurs fois, puis lisez les notes prises par un(e) élève et faites un résumé de quelques lignes en anglais ou en français.

Life for most people = general situation	Transhumanists = new information	Immortality = how to achieve idea	Title + visuals
Life = hard / simple = we live – get sick – die – full stop – nothing we can do	Ben Goertzel + Eray Ozkural + crowd ➡ very smart people think we're close to creating super intelligent AI Hope / idea: Change basis of what it means to be human = goal = digital immortality / improve man in all imaginable respects / within lifetime / definitely going to happen – understand more about universe	Science – technology – build AI system massively smarter than humans – Artificial General Intelligence = AGI	Could we live forever: question about immortality Big Ben ➡ London Baby / young people / hospital / hearse ➡ circle of life? Interview = Ben Goertzel = transhumanist / Eray Ozkural = founder Celestial Cybernetics Artificial General Intelligence Classroom with adults / robot with open brain

2 Lisez le document **2** plusieurs fois avant de lire les notes prises par un(e) élève dans le tableau qui suit.

▶ **DOCUMENT 2**

 DYS

Man as God: 'Frankenstein' Turns 200.

As humans, it is our curse and our blessing to be aware of our own mortality – and to suffer with the loss of our close ones – and, in a broader sense, with the predicament[1] of others.

In 1818, Mary Shelley published the first edition of *Frankenstein, or the Modern Prometheus*, a novel that has captured our collective imagination like few others in history.

5 (…)

Fast-forward 200 years, and the cutting-edge[2] science of our time is now a combination of electricity, digital technology, and genetics. Much has changed since Galvani and Volta – but not the hope of so many to use science to go beyond death, acquiring some sort of immortality by transcending the weakness of the flesh[3]. Transhumanists firmly believe that science will be able to

1. predicament (n.) = condition – 2. cutting-edge (exp.) = very modern – 3. flesh (n): *chair*

10 do this, and fairly soon. Possibly, through genetic manipulation and the cloning of oneself, or through a "brain dump[4]", the transfer of your very own neuronal code into machines capable of storing it and of reigniting the synaptic connections so that you can become "pure spirit" so to speak, a digital disembodied creature, transferable from machine to machine like a piece of software: a modern version of the Resurrection. (…)

15 As of now, there are gigantic scientific roadblocks to any of these pursuits.

This is a very good thing. Mary Shelley cautioned us of the dangers of extending science into realms[5] where we have little control of the outcomes[6]. (…)

Scientific research is irreversible; once a new idea is out, it cannot go back into the bottle. It will be pursued somewhere by some individual or group with dubious moral values.

20 Perhaps Frankenstein's 200th anniversary should be celebrated with a worldwide effort to build safeguards so that scientific research that attempts to create new life, or to modify existing life in fundamental ways, gets regulated and controlled. (…)

Marcello Gleiser, npr.org, January 10th, 2018

4. brain dump (exp.) = transfer of the information from your brain to a computer. – 5. realm (n.) = area – 6. routcome (n.) = result

Source (type of document – date) and topic	article, 2018 *Frankenstein*, the novel, is 200 years old, but the subject – the quest for eternal life and the risks that it entails – is still relevant today.
The novel *Frankenstein*	**Author's message**: cautioned us of the dangers of extending science into realms where we have little control over the results.
Situation today	**Modern science**: electricity, digital technology, genetics **Hope of many**: to use science to go beyond death, acquiring a sort of immortality **How?** genetic manipulation – cloning – brain dumping = transferring your very own neuronal code into machines = you become a digital disembodied creature "pure spirit" **When?** transhumanists believe this will happen soon **Risks**: scientific research could be used by immoral people / people with bad intentions **Advice from writer**: should build safeguards so that scientific research that attempts to create new life or to modify existing life in fundamental ways gets regulated and controlled

3 Utilisez les notes pour écrire un court résumé du texte en anglais.

....

....

....

....

....

....

....

STRATEGY

4 Lisez le document **3** plusieurs fois avant de lire les notes prises par un(e) élève dans le tableau qui suit.

▶ **DOCUMENT 3**

One of the phenomena which had peculiarly attracted my attention was the structure of the human frame, and, indeed, any animal endued[1] with life. Whence[2], I often asked myself, how did the principle of life proceed? It was a bold question, and one which has ever been considered as a mystery; yet with how many things are we upon the brink[3] of 5 becoming acquainted, if cowardice or carelessness did not restrain our inquiries. (…)

After days and nights of incredible labour and fatigue, I succeeded in discovering the cause of generation and life; nay, more, I became myself capable of bestowing[4] animation upon lifeless matter. (…)

Les mots transparents m'aident à comprendre le sens.

1. endue (v.): *doter* – 2. whence (adv.) = from where – 3. upon the brink (exp.) = on the point of – 4. bestow (v.) = give

It was on a dreary night of November that I beheld the accomplishment of my toils. With an
10 anxiety that almost amounted to agony, I collected the instruments of life around me, that I might infuse a spark of being into the lifeless thing that lay at my feet. It was already one in the morning; the rain pattered dismally against the panes[5], and my candle was nearly burnt out, when, by the glimmer of the half-extinguished light, I saw the dull yellow eye of the creature open; it breathed hard, and a convulsive motion agitated its limbs.

15 How can I describe my emotions at this catastrophe, or how delineate the wretch[6] whom with such infinite pains and care I had endeavoured[7] to form? His limbs were in proportion, and I had selected his features as beautiful. Beautiful! Great God! (…)

The different accidents of life are not so changeable as the feelings of human nature. I had worked hard
20 for nearly two years, for the sole purpose of infusing life into an inanimate body. For this I had deprived myself of rest and health. I had desired it with an ardour that far exceeded moderation; but now that I had finished, the beauty of the dream vanished, and breathless horror and disgust filled my heart.

Mary Wollestonecraft Shelley, *Frankenstein or the Modern Prometheus*, 1818

5. pane (n.): *vitre* – 6. wretch (n.) = miserable creature – 7. endeavour (v.) = try

Source (type of document, date, title, author…)	literary (fantasy / science fiction), extract from novel, written by Mary Wollestonecraft Shelley in 1818 = + 200 years old
Main subject	After a lot of hard work, the narrator creates a human life and he is appalled at the result.
About the narrator and his creation	**Probable profession**: doctor, scientist **Original interest / question**: the structure of the human / animal body – how was life formed? **Narrator while making his creation (opinion / feelings / characteristics)**: obsessed with creation of life = *"often asked myself,"*, *"deprived myself of rest and health"*, – determined / dedicated = *"incredible labour and fatigue"*; *"had worked hard for nearly two years"* **Description of creation**: *"dull yellow eye"*, *"creature"* = animal-like; *"the wretch"* – *"his limbs were in proportion"*, *"I had selected his features as beautiful. Beautiful! Great God!"* ➔ ugly **Narrator's feelings after creation**: disappointed: *"the beauty of the dream vanished"* – horrified and disgusted: *"breathless horror and disgust filled my heart"*

5 Utilisez les notes de cet(te) élève pour écrire un résumé du texte en anglais.

....
....
....
....
....
....

🔺 Practise

6 Appuyez-vous sur les notes et les résumés que vous avez faits pour identifier les points communs des trois documents.

> Je surligne dans mes notes les points communs en utilisant différentes couleurs (une couleur par point commun).

Links between documents 1, 2 and 3.

....
....
....
....
....

....
....
....
....

7 Analysez la consigne d'examen ci-dessous, puis complétez la carte mentale avec une ou deux citations des trois documents.

> Using all three documents, discuss the significance of immortality for humans.

Docs 1+2+3

Different opinions on the mysteries of life, death and immortality, on what we should or shouldn't do. However, it's always been a significant topic for humans.

....
....
....
....

Docs 2+3

In 1818, Mary Shelley based her novel on the subject of immortality. The main character works on making a body come to life. The author wanted to warn people against this.

....
....
....
....
....

Docs 1+2+3

Mortality is a fact all humans have to deal with.

....
....
....

Significance of immortality

Docs 2+3

The question of immortality is not a new one ➡ humans have been fascinated by the idea for many years.

....
....
....
....

Docs 1+2

Some people, who call themselves transhumanists, don't accept that mortality is inevitable.

....
....
....
....
....

STRATEGY

Have a go

ÉVALUATION 1   ÉVALUATION 2   ÉVALUATION 3

➤ **EXAM PREP • 116-127**

8 Répondez à la question suivante sur feuille séparée en utilisant les stratégies ci-dessus (120 mots au moins).

Using all three documents, explain the potential and risks of uncontrolled scientific research.

Créer des liens : écrire ou parler à partir d'une image

bordos Flash **PAGE** audio

⬤ Observe and analyse

① **Faites une analyse rapide de l'image à l'aide du guidage et des amorces en italique.**

Carrie Mae Weems, *Untitled* (*Open Book With Daughter*), from *Kitchen Table* Series, 1990

Main elements: What? (nature, context) Who? (author) Who for? (addressee)
It's a… / It was taken from, it's entitled, painted / taken by… It's aimed at…

....
....
....
....
....

Description: Structure (right, left, centre, focal point, etc.). People. Objects. Places. Point of view
It shows… / in the foreground, background, centre, she looks, the colours, shades, shadows…

....
....
....
....
....
....
....

Implicit meaning: People (type, social origin). Relationship. A theme / an idea / a link / an event
Maybe, it could be, I guess, she seems, she must be…

....
....

Interpretation:
Purpose: artistic – inform – make us think – illustrate
She aims at + V-ing / may want to make us… / What she probably wanted to highlight was…

....
....

Creator's intention – possible meaning: *I find it + adj., what I find, to me it is…*

....
....

My opinion: *I can't help thinking / it makes me think of / it reminds me of / it could be related to / it's quite close to / we can deduce that…*

....
....
....
....

IN A WORD

Une image a toujours un **sens explicite** (= dénoté) et un **sens implicite** (= connoté). Que ce soit à l'écrit ou à l'oral, **montrer** qu'on a bien **compris le sens véhiculé** par l'image est **un plus**.

2 Observez ces deux sujets type bac (écrit et oral) et soulignez les mots qui font le lien avec l'image. Prenez des notes sur ce que vous constatez pour chaque type d'évaluation.

> To what extent does this picture illustrate the importance of education for women?

> Expliquez en quoi cette image illustre l'axe *Espace privé* et *espace public*.

> Je lis le sujet en m'interrogeant sur les attentes précises du jury avant de me lancer.

À l'écrit : ....

À l'oral : ....

 Practise

The fire season of January 2020 was one of the worst in Australia's history, hundreds of homes were destroyed and millions of acres burned. Here, a kangaroo rushes past a burning house in Lake Conjola, New South Wales, Australia.

3 Entraînez-vous à répondre au sujet en écrivant un texte de 120 mots minimum à partir de l'image ci-dessus.

> To what extent does this picture illustrate the natural disaster wildfires represent? What is your personal position on the question?

> Je me sers de la légende pour comprendre la portée de cette image.

STRATEGY

> **Examples:** for instance – like – such as – to illustrate – according to
> **Transitions:** first of all – then – next – in addition – moreover – furthermore – last but not least – finally
> **Linkwords:** however – on the other hand – nevertheless – as / since – whereas – as opposed to...
> **Personal opinion:** I find it + *adj.*, what I find, to me it is...

4 Entraînez-vous à parler pendant cinq minutes à partir de l'image pour expliquer en quoi elle illustre l'axe *Innovations scientifiques et responsabilité*. Écoutez un exemple de production orale.

> **Structure:** first and foremost – let's move on to – then – what's more – to conclude

> **Opinion:** I can't help thinking / It makes me think of / It reminds me of / It could be related to / It's quite close to...

> **Gap-fillers:** well – I mean – you know

Créer des liens : écrire ou parler à partir d'une citation ▶ 89, 94

bordas
Flash
PAGE
audio

🔴 Observe and analyse

Les mots-clés vous permettent d'identifier le sens global de la citation. Les citations sont souvent très denses et nécessitent une explicitation du sens implicite.

> "When asked what attribute he most admired in human nature, Mahatma Gandhi replied, simply and immediately, 'Courage'. 'Nonviolence', he said, 'is not to be used ever as the shield of the coward. It is the weapon of the brave."
>
> **Lord Richard Attenborough,**
> film director and producer
> (his film *Gandhi* swept the Oscars in 1983)

Il est important de bien identifier le point de vue exprimé (subjectif, objectif, d'une personne célèbre, etc.).

Le nom de l'auteur et la source permettent de contextualiser la citation. Il faut les prendre en compte dans l'analyse.

💡 Je m'appuie sur les mots-clés, les images, les métaphores pour émettre des hypothèses de sens. Parfois plusieurs interprétations sont possibles, je n'hésite pas à les donner.

1 Soulignez tous les mots-clés qui vous semblent importants dans la citation et dans la source.

2 Complétez le tableau pour faire une analyse rapide de la citation à l'aide du guidage proposé :

	Writing about a text
Presenting the quotation (source, author, point of view)	This quotation is ....
Reformulating the main idea → explicit and implicit meaning	It deals with ....
Giving your opinion	I believe ....

💡 Je cherche des exemples et des illustrations pour développer la citation avant de donner mon avis personnel.

refer to /
allude to
It could be
argued that /
it is true that...
on the one /
other hand...
for example /
for instance: ...

IN A WORD **Une citation s'analyse :** il faudra ensuite **montrer** par la **reformulation** qu'on a compris le **sens explicite** et **implicite** avant de **développer** le sujet.

3 Observez ces deux sujets type bac (écrit et oral). Prenez des notes sur ce que vous constatez pour chaque type d'évaluation.

Expression écrite : *Comment on these words by Gandhi:* "Non-violence is not to be used ever as the shield of the coward. It is the weapon of the brave."

Expression orale en continu : parlez pendant cinq minutes à partir de cette citation en montrant en quoi elle illustre l'axe 5 du programme *Fictions et réalités.*
"Non-violence is not to be used ever as the shield of the coward. It is the weapon of the brave."

À l'écrit : ....
....
....

À l'oral : ....
....

💡 Pour l'oral, je pense aux mots-clés liés à chaque axe du programme pour m'aider à trouver des idées.

ÉVALUATION 1 | ÉVALUATION 2 | ÉVALUATION 3

➤ EXAM PREP • 104-127

4 Vous traiterez en anglais et en 120 mots au moins le sujet suivant.

Who do you relate to more and why?

"With languages, you are at home anywhere."
Edmund De Waal, contemporary English artist and author

"Learning another language is not only learning different words for the same things, but learning another way to think about things."
Flora Lewis, journalist, 1922-2002

Although both quotations are relevant my preference goes to...
One of the main reasons why I can relate more to X is...

It seems patently clear to me that
We should nonetheless remember that...
Not everyone has the possibility to...

5 Choisissez la citation qui illustre le mieux à votre sens l'axe *Diversité et inclusion*. Vous disposez de cinq minutes pour présenter et expliquer votre choix sans lire vos notes. Écoutez ensuite les deux élèves qui parlent de la citation qu'ils ont choisie.

"I speak not for myself but for those without a voice... those who have fought for their rights, their right to live in peace, their right to be treated with dignity, their right for equality of opportunity, their right to be educated."
Malala Yousafzai, co-recipient of the 2014 Nobel Peace Prize

"A Nation should not be judged by how it treats its highest citizens, but its lowest ones."
Nelson Mandela, 1st black president of South Africa, in: *Long Walk to Freedom* (autobiography)

Je m'entraîne en m'enregistrant pour pouvoir me réécouter.

I find it + adj / what I find / to me it is...
There's a clear link between... – The point he / she makes echoes...
The reason I have chosen the second quotation is...
Another thing that strikes me is...

STRATEGY

Expressions utiles

À l'écrit et à l'oral

Introduire

The main topic is…
The main characters are…
The text / video / recording covers the issue of…
The story / scene is set in…
The article deals with…

Commencer

(…) is a popular topic / much talked about these days.
The first thing that comes to mind when I see / read this is…
Before getting to the heart of the subject, I'd like to begin by…

Citer

As (…) once remarked / pointed out…
According to (…), and I quote, …
To quote X…

Commenter

Given the situation it seems likely / unlikely / inevitable that…
What's striking is that….
When the narrator says… he / she implies that…
What is suggested is that…

Réagir à une citation

I've chosen to talk about the first / second quotation…
The reason I think this quotation is particularly apt is…
What I find appealing in this quotation is…
I can only agree with X when he / she states…
Although both quotations are relevant my preference goes to…
The point he / she makes echoes…

Lier à un axe

There is a clear link between X and the theme…
This quotation immediately evokes the theme…
Reading this quotation made me think about the theme…
We can draw a parallel between the subject of this photo and the theme…

Donner un exemple

For instance, …
For example, …
Such as…

Justifier

I say that because…
This can be justified by the fact that…
What makes this patently clear is that….
This idea is backed up by…

Se focaliser sur un point

If we focus on… what we notice is…
I'd like to draw your attention to…
Zooming in on… it becomes apparent that…
A close examination of… brings to light the fact that…

À l'oral

Reformuler

If I can rephrase that…
The main idea here is that…
In other words, …
What I'm trying to say is…

Réagir à une remarque

I've never thought about it that way before.
Good point!
I get your / his / her / their point.
I see what he / she means / you mean.
I think that's highly unlikely.

Annoncer un plan
I'd like to begin by talking about…
In the first place / First and foremost I'd like to…
I will then move on to my next point, which deals with…
Following that, I will discuss…
This will bring me to my conclusion, which will serve to…

Donner son opinion
The way I see it, …
In my opinion…
As far as I'm concerned…
It seems to me that…
I (really) feel that…
In my opinion…

Exprimer son accord / désaccord et nuancer
I fully / completely / wholeheartedly agree/ disagree / with…
We are not on the same page about…
That's (exactly) the way I feel.
I can only agree with X when he / she states…
I see what you mean but…
I agree with you to a certain extent / up to a point but…

Expliquer
What they mean by that is…
The point they're trying to make is…
What we can gather is that…

Faire une transition
Moving on to our next point…
Now that we've dealt with… the next point I'd like to bring up is…

Organiser
To begin I'd like to…
As my next point…
Once we have discussed… it would be useful to move on to…
Before finishing we could…
Last but not least…

Reprendre un point
As I stated earlier…
To get back to the point I was making…
Coming back to our original point…

Ajouter
In addition, …
What's more…
Furthermore…
Secondly / Thirdly…
Lastly

Conclure
To sum up…
To recap…
In conclusion, …
To conclude…

Demander à répéter
Sorry, I didn't catch that.
Could you repeat that, please?
Sorry, I missed that. Could you say it again, please?
Could you run that by me one more time, please?

Gérer les hésitations
How can I put it – Actually – You know – I mean… – You know what I mean – Let me explain – Let me clarify – Well, what I'm trying to say is…

Évaluation 1

2e trimestre de Première [20 points]

▲ SUJET 1 Axe 3 Art et pouvoir

(Compréhension de l'oral) ▶ 46-53

🎧 ▶ **Titre du document** *New Banksy Mural Shines Light on Homelessness.*
Source : *Inside Edition*, **December 10th, 2019**

En rendant compte en français du document, vous montrerez que vous avez identifié et compris :

VIDÉO

- la nature et le thème principal du document ;
- le déroulement des faits, la situation, les événements, les informations ;
- l'identité des personnes ou personnages et, éventuellement, les liens entre elles / eux ;
- les éventuels différents points de vue ;
- la fonction et la portée du document (relater, informer, convaincre, critiquer, dénoncer).

> 💡 Pour m'aider à comprendre, j'observe attentivement les différentes œuvres de Banksy.

....
....
....
....
....
....
....
....
....
....
....

▲ SUJET 2 Axe 1 Identités et échanges

(Compréhension de l'oral) ▶ 46-51

AUDIO

🎧 ▶ **Titre du document** *Santiago Potes Is 1st Latino DACA Recipient To Be Awarded Rhodes Scholarship*
Source : **NPR (National Public Radio), "Morning Edition", December 8th , 2020**

Vous rendrez compte en français de ce que vous avez compris du document.

> 💡 Le mot *Columbia* apparaît deux fois et se réfère à deux lieux : je me concentre sur le contexte pour comprendre lesquels.

....
....
....
....
....
....
....
....
....
....

🔵 **SUJET 3** Axe 4 Citoyenneté et mondes virtuels

bordas
Flash
PAGE
audio

Compréhension de l'oral ▶ 46-51

▶ **Titre du document** *Managing Misinformation on News Aggregation Site Reddit*

Source : **NPR (National Public Radio), December 8th, 2019**

AUDIO

En rendant compte en français du document, vous montrerez que vous avez identifié et compris :

- la nature et le thème principal du document ;
- le déroulement des faits, la situation, les événements, les informations ;
- l'identité des personnes et, éventuellement, les liens entre elles / eux ;
- les éventuels différents points de vue ;
- les éventuels éléments implicites du document ;
- la fonction et la portée du document (relater, informer, convaincre, critiquer, dénoncer, etc.).

> 💡 Le titre m'indique que je vais entendre parler de réseaux sociaux.

....
....
....
....
....
....
....
....
....

🔵 **SUJET 4** Axe 2 Espace privé et espace public

bordas
Flash
PAGE
vidéo

Compréhension de l'oral ▶ 46-51

AUDIO

▶ **Titre du document** *People Working from Home Permanently Could Transform Rural America*

Source : **NPR (National Public Radio), "Morning Edition", April 5th, 2021**

Vous rendrez compte en français de ce que vous avez compris du document.

> 💡 Je ne cherche pas forcément à comprendre tous les noms propres : ils ne sont pas toujours essentiels à la reformulation du sens.

....
....
....
....
....
....
....
....
....

EXAM PREP

Évaluation 1
2e trimestre de Première [20 points]

🔺 SUJET 5 Axe 6 Innovations scientifiques et responsabilité

bordas
Flash PAGE
audio

(Compréhension de l'oral) ▶ 46-51

🎧 ▶ **Titre du document** *The Reasons Kids Aren't Getting Vaccinations.*
Source : **NPR (National Public Radio), "All things considered", May 20th, 2019**

En rendant compte en français du document, vous montrerez que vous avez identifié et compris :

AUDIO
- la nature et le thème principal du document ;
- le déroulement des faits, la situation, les événements, les informations ;
- l'identité des personnes ou personnages et, éventuellement, les liens entre elles / eux ;
- les éventuels différents points de vue ;
- les éventuels éléments implicites du document ;
- la fonction et la portée du document (relater, informer, convaincre, critiquer, dénoncer, etc.).

> 💡 Je m'appuie sur le champ lexical médical pour deviner que *measles* est une maladie infantile.

....
....
....
....
....
....
....
....
....

🔺 SUJET 6 Axe 5 Fictions et réalités

bordas
Flash PAGE
vidéo

(Compréhension de l'oral) ▶ 46-51

AUDIO
▶ **Titre du document** *Lawrence Wright Wishes His Pandemic Novel* **The End of October** *Had Gotten It Wrong*
Source : **NPR (National Public Radio), "All Things Considered", April 28th, 2020**

> 💡 Je m'appuie sur les dates de la source et celles évoquées dans le document sonore pour situer les événements.

Vous rendrez compte en français de ce que vous avez compris du document.

....
....
....
....
....
....
....
....
....
....

⏺ SUJET 7 Axe 8 Territoire et mémoire

bordas Flash PAGE video

Compréhension de l'oral ▶ 46-53

VIDÉO

▶ **Titre du document** *Danny Boyle Captures the Spirit of Armistice Day.*

Source : **Sky News, October 5th, 2018**

> 💡 Je m'appuie sur les images pour comprendre en quoi la personne interviewée est célèbre.

Vous rendrez compte, en français, de ce que vous avez compris du document.

....

....

....

....

....

....

....

....

....

⏺ SUJET 8 Axe 7 Diversité et inclusion

bordas Flash PAGE vidéo

Compréhension de l'oral ▶ 46-51

▶ **Titre du document** *A Racist Encounter Inspired Two Teens Jeenah Gwak and Hope Yu to Publish a Magazine on the AAPI (Asian Americans and Pacific Islanders) Experience*

Source : **NPR (National Public Radio), May 21st, 2021**

> 💡 Je m'appuie sur les mots accentués et je les classe par thématiques en m'aidant de ce que j'ai pu anticiper grâce au titre.

En rendant compte du document en français, vous montrerez que vous avez identifié et compris :

AUDIO

- la nature et le thème principal du document ;
- la situation, les événements, les informations ;
- les personnes, leur fonction ou leur rôle, et le cas échéant, leurs points de vue et la tonalité (comique, ironique, lyrique, polémique, etc.) de leurs propos ;
- le but, la fonction du document (relater, informer, convaincre, critiquer, dénoncer, divertir, etc.).

....

....

....

....

....

....

....

....

....

....

....

....

....

EXAM PREP

Évaluation 2 – Sujet 1

3ᵉ trimestre de Première 20 points

Le sujet porte sur l'**axe 1** du programme : **Identités et échanges**.

① Compréhension de l'écrit   3 647 signes   ▶ 54-67, 90

▶ **Text 1**

 DYS

Autumn 1945, New York.

(…) Delia and her mother are alone. Alone as on that day, up in her attic practice room, when Delia first spoke about the man she'd fallen for. How fine her mother had been, after the first shock.

(…) "I'm so tired, Mama." (…)

5 "I'm tired of everybody thinking they know what colored means."

(…) "Who's telling you that? Nobody here's going to tell you what colored means."

(…) "My boys are… different."

"Look around you, girl. Everybody here's different. Different's the commonest thing going."

"I've got to give them the freedom to be –"

10 Her mother pinches up her face. "Don't you dare talk to me about your freedom. Your brother died in the war – for that word. A black man, fighting to give folks in other countries a freedom he wouldn't ever've had in his own, even if he came back here alive."

"Lots of people died in the war, Mama. White people. Black people. Yellow people."(…)

"It's not one thing against the other. We're not taking anything away. Just giving. Giving them
15 space, choice, the right to make a lifetime anywhere among –"

"This why you married a white man? So you could make babies light enough to do what they wouldn't let you do?" (…) "White's just one color. Black's everything else. You gonna raise them to have a choice? That choice don't belong to them. Everybody else is going to make it for them!"

(…) "What are you going to tell them to call themselves?"

20 "Mama. That's the point. We're not calling them anything. That way they'll never have to call another person –"

"White? You raising them white?"

"Don't be silly. We're trying to raise them… beyond race."

Richard Powers, *The Time of Our Singing*, 2003

▶ **Text 2**

 DYS

White kids, racism and the way privileged parenting props up an unjust system.

This past October, my son and his classmates lobbied their small private school to change the official holiday of Columbus Day to Native People's Day. My son wrote a short letter to the faculty explaining why they shouldn't celebrate white imperialism, and that native peoples were too often ignored or erased or pushed to the side in discussions of American history. Some parents didn't like
5 the change, but the teachers and administration were supportive, and they changed the name.

As you'd imagine, my wife and I were very proud. We'd hoped to teach our son anti-racism, and here he was doing anti-racist activism in his own small way. We were glad we'd sent him to a school that encouraged kids to speak up, and was open to change.

At the same time, though, the school is a private school. Sending kids to private school is an option you
10 only have if you have a certain amount of money. (…) And affluent people in the U.S. are often (though not always) white. We sent our son to a school that taught and encouraged anti-racism. But teaching people to be anti-racist doesn't necessarily address the structure of racism itself. In fact, racist structures often determine who does and does not have access to these kinds of educational opportunities. (…)

Margaret Hagerman, a sociologist at Mississippi State University, talks about these difficult
15 contradictions in her book, "White Kids: Growing Up with Privilege in a Racially Divided America."
(…) Some parents, Hagerman found, preferred to keep race unspoken. Families she interviewed in
a wealthy, conservative suburb, for example, tended to avoid the topic of race with their children.
"They adhered to a color blind way of thinking," Hagerman told me. "They would say that race
doesn't matter, or that we're beyond race." One girl told Hagerman that in her school, they weren't
20 even allowed to say the word "racist" – it was on a list of forbidden words that also included
homophobic, sexist, and racist slurs.

Noah Berlatsky, nbcnews.com, January, 2nd, 2019

Give an account in English and in your own words of text 1 and then of text 2.

▶ **In your account of text 1:**

Le champ lexical des couleurs est un bon indice pour trouver le thème principal de ce texte.

a. Present the two main characters and the main topic of the text.

....
....
....
....
....
....
....
....
....
....
....
....

b. Focus on the following three clues and explain what they reveal about Delia's feelings / opinion.
Explain what opposes Delia to her mother.
 – "Giving them space, choice, the right to make a lifetime anywhere" (line 14, paragraph 10);
 – "We're not calling them anything." (line 20, paragraph 13);
 – "We're trying to raise them… beyond race." (line 23, paragraph 15).

....
....
....

Pour trouver le point de vue de la mère, je relis les passages où elle intervient et j'en déduis son sentiment.

....
....
....
....
....
....
....
....

EXAM PREP

> **In your account of text 2:**

c. Present Noah Berlatsky and his wife.

....
....
....
....

d. Explain the parents' educational choices and their son's attitude.

....
....
....
....
....
....
....
....

e. Comment on the last paragraph and explain what is particular about some families' point of view.

....
....
....
....
....
....

After your accounts of text 1 and 2, answer the following question:

f. What theme do the two texts have in common and, in relation to this theme, what are the similarities and differences between the two experiences?

....
....
....
....
....
....
....
....
....
....
....
....

② Expression écrite ▶ 68-71, 78, 83, 98

Vous traiterez en anglais l'un des deux sujets suivants au choix. Répondez en 120 mots au moins.

● **Sujet A**

Your school has decided to take part in a project to promote individuality: "Don't label me!" Write a message on your school website to give your opinion.

● **Sujet B**

To what extent can education contribute to more equality between people from different origins?

Évaluation 2 – Sujet 2

3ᵉ trimestre de Première   20 points

 bordas Flash PAGE · PDF DYS

L'ensemble du sujet porte sur **l'axe 3** du programme : **Art et pouvoir**.

1 Compréhension de l'écrit · 2 847 signes ▶ 54-61

 DYS

The great highways streamed with moving people. There in the Middle–and Southwest had lived a simple agrarian folk who had not changed with industry, who had not farmed with machines or known the power and danger of machines in private hands. (…)

And then suddenly the machines pushed them out and they swarmed on the highways. The movement
5   changed them; the highways, the camps along the road, the fear of hunger and the hunger itself, changed them. The children without dinner changed them, the endless moving changed them. They were migrants. (…)

In the West there was panic when the migrants multiplied on the highways. Men of property were terrified for their property. Men who had never been hungry saw the eyes of the hungry. Men who
10   had never wanted anything very much saw the flare of want in the eyes of the migrants. And the men of the towns and of the soft suburban country gathered to defend themselves; and they reassured themselves that they were good and the invaders bad, as a man must do before he fights. They said, These goddamned Okies are dirty and ignorant. They're degenerate, sexual maniacs. Those goddamned Okies are thieves. They'll steal anything. They've got no sense of property rights.

15   And the latter was true, for how can a man without property know the ache of ownership? And the defending people said, They bring disease, they're filthy. We can't have them in the schools. They're strangers. How'd you like to have your sister go out with one of 'em?

(…)

And the migrants streamed in on the highways and their hunger was in their eyes, and their need was
20   in their eyes. They had no argument, no system, nothing but their numbers and their needs. When there was work for a man, ten men fought for it – fought with a low wage. If that fella'll work for thirty cents, I'll work for twenty-five.

If he'll take twenty-five, I'll do it for twenty.

No, me, I'm hungry. I'll work for fifteen. I'll work for food. The kids. You ought to see them. Little
25   boils, like, comin' out, an' they can't run aroun'. Give 'em some windfall fruit, an' they bloated up. Me, I'll work for a little piece of meat.

And this was good, for wages went down and prices stayed up. The great owners were glad and they sent out more handbills to bring more people in. And wages went down and prices stayed up. And pretty soon now we'll have serfs again.

30   (…) The fields were fruitful, and starving men moved on the roads. The granaries were full and the children of the poor grew up rachitic, and the pustules of pellagra swelled on their sides. The great companies did not know that the line between hunger and anger is a thin line. And money that might have gone to wages went for gas, for guns, for agents and spies, for blacklists, for drilling. On the highways the people moved like ants and searched for work, for food. And the anger began to ferment.

John Steinbeck, *The Grapes of Wrath*, 1939

> Je regarde la date et j'identifie le genre du texte avant de commencer à le lire.

Answer the following questions **in English**, using your own words.

a. After reading the text, what can you say about:

– the main topic of the text and the population that is described;

....

....

....

....

– their original home, their destination and their travelling conditions;

....
....
....
....

– why they are in this situation and how it affects them;

....
....
....
....
....

b. Focus on the following clues:
   – "These goddamed Okies are dirty and ignorant." (line 13, paragraph 3);
   – "We can't have them in the schools." (line 16, paragraph 4);
   – "How'd you like to have your sister go out with one of 'em?" (line 17, paragraph 4).

What do they reveal about the people who say this? Explain why they react this way. Quote from the text to justify.

....
....
....
....
....
....
....
....
....
....
....

c. Focus on what is said about the 'wages' (paragraphs 5-7). Explain what happened. Quote from the text to justify.

....
....
....
....
....
....
....
....
....

d. Comment on the following sentence and explain what is implied: 'The great companies did not know that the line between hunger and anger is a thin line.'

....
....
....
....

EXAM PREP

2 Expression écrite ▶ 68-71, 76, 83, 94, 98

Vous traiterez en anglais l'un des deux sujets suivants au choix. Répondez en 120 mots au moins.

● **Sujet A**

Your school will receive a group of migrants for a three-month stay in order to help them settle in your country. Write a message for the school blog to explain the situation and inform the families.

● **Sujet B**

It's 1936 and you are a reporter. You were with Dorothea Lange when she took this photo and you met the people we see in it. Write a short article.

> J'observe attentivement la photo et j'imagine ce que doivent ressentir les personnes que je vois.

Dorothea Lange, Family between Dallas and Austin, August 1936

Évaluation 2 – Sujet 3
3ᵉ trimestre de Première  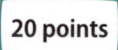 20 points

L'ensemble du sujet porte sur **l'axe 8** du programme : **Territoire et mémoire**.

1 **Compréhension de l'écrit** 2 752 signes ▶ 54, 62

DYS

Irish famine film *Black 47* wins over the critics

Filmmakers have long steered clear of the Irish famine, a trauma of starvation, poverty and suffering that remains a sacred national topic. It seemed too bleak, too depressing, too fraught – get a historical detail wrong and you risked accusations of insensitivity and exploitation.

Now, 170 years after a million people died and more than a million emigrated, comes *Black 47*,
5 a big-screen blockbuster that uses the famine as a western-style revenge thriller. There are lots of muskets, explosions and horse chases, the lead actors are Australian, and many of the interiors were shot in Luxembourg.

And the Irish love it. Cinemagoers flocked to the film's opening weekend, making it the biggest grossing Irish film in Ireland this year with a box office of €444,000 (£395,000).

10 (…)

The $10m Irish-Luxembourgian co-production is set for a North American premiere at the Toronto International Film Festival this week before opening in the UK and US on 28 September.

It stars James Frecheville as an Irish ranger who returns home in 1847 after fighting for the British army in Afghanistan and discovers that his mother has died of hunger, his brother has been hanged,
15 and the rest of his family is inhabiting a wasteland of ruined crops and official callousness in Connemara on the Atlantic coast.

When the ranger launches a campaign of bloody vengeance against authority, the British draft one of his former comrades, played by Hugo Weaving, to track him down.

Jim Broadbent plays Lord Kilmichael, an aristocrat who exports grain despite corpses piling up in
20 the countryside, and Stephen Rea plays a Gaelic / English translator. Freddie Fox, Barry Keoghan, Moe Dunford, and Sarah Greene also star.

"The famine is one of those essential Irish stories that we haven't figured out a way to bring to the screen," the director, Lance Daly, told *The Guardian* on Monday. "Doing it as a revenge thriller was a really smart way to smuggle the story of the great hunger to a wide audience which might not
25 be first in line to watch a film about famine and suffering and the truly horrid history of the time."

Daly, from Dublin, filmed the exteriors in Connemara and Wicklow and consulted historians on the details.

The famine, triggered by a blight[1] in potato crops, ravaged Ireland from 1845 to 1849, a humanitarian catastrophe that flummoxed the British government even as Quakers, Native American Choctaws,
30 the Ottoman empire and others sent assistance.

"It's not just some story," said Daly. "It's a story that belongs to everyone. I felt a great responsibility to get the history right, to get the language right, and that didn't make the British characters out to be villains and the Irish as innocent victims. The deeper you go, the more complex it gets." (…)

Roy Carrol, theguardian.com, September 17ᵗʰ, 2018

1. blight (n.) = illness

Account for the text **in English** taking into consideration its nature and main topic, the causes and consequences of the Irish famine and how Irish people feel about it today and react to its portrayal in films.

Je fais le tri entre les faits historiques et ce qui a été inventé pour le film.

② **Expression écrite** ▶ 68-73, 83, 94, 98

Vous traiterez en anglais l'un des deux sujets suivants au choix. Répondez en 120 mots au moins.

● **Sujet A**

Your school is organising a 'History Day' to commemorate different historical events that have shaped the world. Write a post on the forum of the school blog to say which event you would like to commemorate and why.

> Je fais une liste d'événements possibles et je choisis celui que je maîtrise le mieux.

● **Sujet B**

You are Billy / Mary. You're visiting Dublin and you come across the famine memorial. Send an email to your American penfriend, along with this photo that you took.

The Famine Statues, presented to Dublin in 1997 by sculptor **Rowan Gillespie**, commemorate the Great Famine of the mid-19th century.

New message

From
To
Subject

Send   A 🔗 😊 🖼   ⋮ 🗑

Évaluation 3 – Sujet 1 [20 points]

3e trimestre de Terminale

PARTIE 1 – Écrit

L'ensemble du sujet porte sur l'**axe 2** du programme : **Espace privé et espace public**.

1 Compréhension de l'oral ▶ 46-51

> **Document 1** ***Ride-hailing Services Like Uber or Lyft Are Contributing to Traffic and Pollution Problem.***
>
> Source : **NPR (National Public Radio), "Morning Edition", August 1st, 2018**

Je repère les chiffres pour avoir des données précises à citer dans mon compte-rendu.

En rendant compte, **en français**, du document, vous montrerez que vous avez identifié et compris :

AUDIO
- sa nature et son thème principal ;
- les personnes qui s'expriment et leur témoignage ;
- la fonction et la portée du document (relater, informer, convaincre, critiquer, dénoncer, etc.).

....

....

....

....

....

....

....

....

2 Compréhension de l'écrit (3 438 signes) et de l'ensemble du dossier

▶ 54-67, 90

> **Document 2**

DYS

Freddy, a driver with both Uber and Lyft, pulls into the parking lot when he comes to pick me up, giving me a moment to search out his large sedan on a bright day in Atlanta, Georgia. With more than three years of vagrant sociology research under my belt, I've learned to hop into cars on busy streets as soon as I recognize the vehicle's license plate from my smartphone screen. (…)

5   Freddy tells me he's a twelve-year veteran of the army, having left around 1989, just before the Gulf War. I explain to him that I'm not just another passenger; I'm a researcher studying how Uber and technology affect work. As I ask him basic questions, he tells me that he also works full time as the manager of a fast-food restaurant in a nearby city. When he has time off from his primary job, he commutes three hours into Atlanta to take ridehail jobs. During his vacation period, he spends about four days working ridehail jobs,
10 heads home for a day or two and then returns to the lineup of drivers waiting for ride requests in the airport parking lot. "We have a quale (queue), a place where all the Uber and Lyft drivers park, and I stay there." His sister lives not too far away, and that's where he showers.

When I ask him where he sleeps in between driving shifts, he nods to the front passenger seat and exclaims, "You're sitting in my bed!" With a reassuring smile, he adds that he's not the only one who does it – men and
15 women from outside the city are catching up on sleep in the airport parking lot. Sometimes he works fourteen to sixteen hours in a single day, and the next day he'll do eight hours, depending on how he feels. He aims to average two hundred dollars a day, and on this trip, he's proud to be earning "double money"– his vacation pay from his fast-food job supplements whatever he makes driving. "During the vacation period, I really had nothing to do," he says, "and I'm a people person, I love meeting new people."

20 As in the case of many of the people I've met during my research, driving is a second job for Freddy, and he genuinely enjoys the social connection he gains from conversations with passengers.

Alex Rosenblat, UBERLAND, 2018

▶ Document 3

"I made \$3.75 an hour": Lyft and Uber drivers push to unionize for better pay.

For over a year Rob Mead has worked as an Uber driver in Reno, Nevada, to supplement his income as a public sector worker. Now he's wondering if it is worth it. "After gas, added monthly rideshare insurance, wear-and-tear, constant oil changes and taxes that \$300 for 30 hours of work I thought I made in a week actually averages down to about \$90 after expenses," said Mead.

5 "A few weeks ago I drove four passengers in a one-hour period. I looked at my profits and I made only \$12. It was snowing, traffic was crazy and I basically risked my life to make that \$12. After expenses I made \$3.75 that entire hour." (…)

Uber and Lyft are planning to give some long-term drivers money to buy stock (…). But only a minority will be eligible and in the meantime drivers are organizing for better wages rather than
10 bonuses.

"I'm not interested in what stingy package they're going to offer," said James Hicks, an Uber driver in Los Angeles for about four years. He has not heard anything from Uber regarding stock grants for drivers, but said he had recently had his pay slashed by the company. "You can't tell me a billion-dollar company can't afford to pay their drivers when all they really need to worry about is
15 marketing and upkeep of the app."

Michael Sainato, theguardian.com, March 22nd, 2019

a. Compréhension du document 2.

Give an account of document 2 **in English** and in your own words, paying particular attention to:
- the narrator and his relationship with Freddie;
- Freddie and the difference between his two jobs;
- Freddie's reasons for having a second job.

b. Compréhension du document 3.

Give an account of document 2 **in English** and in your own words, paying particular attention to:
- the main topic of the text;
- the people interviewed;
- their feelings about the situation;
- the references to money and how they illustrate the main problem;
- the companies' suggested solution with that of the drivers;
- James Hicks' point of view at the end of the text (l. 13-15, paragraphe 4).

....

....

....

....

....

....

....

....

> Je cherche le point commun entre tous les chiffres de ce texte pour dégager le message véhiculé.

c. Compréhension de l'ensemble du dossier.

Consider the three documents (1, 2, 3) and explain the positive and negative aspects of ride-hailing services.

....

....

....

....

....

....

....

> Je prépare un brouillon avec un tableau à deux colonnes avant de rédiger afin de bien penser à évoquer les aspects positifs et négatifs pris dans les trois documents.

③ Expression écrite ▸ 68-71, 82, 83, 88-93, 98

Vous traiterez en anglais l'un des deux sujets suivants au choix. Répondez en 120 mots au moins.

● **Sujet A**

Which opinion do you feel closer to? Explain your choice with clear examples.

> I'd never use ride-hailing services as they exploit their drivers and increase pollution.

> I think it's great to be able to take a taxi at a reasonable price. And people aren't forced to work for them. It's all about freedom of choice.

● **Sujet B**

You are an Uber driver and you have just come home after a day protesting about your working conditions. Write about your day in your diary – the reasons for your protest, the people you met, the conversations you had, your thoughts and feelings...

....

....

....

....

....

....

....

....

....

....

....

....

....

Partie 2 - Oral

1 Expression orale en continu ▶ 84, 87, 96-99

Choisissez parmi les documents A et B celui qui illustre le mieux, à votre sens, l'axe *Espace privé et espace public*. Vous disposez de **10 minutes de préparation**. Puis **présentez et expliquez votre choix** en parlant pendant **cinq minutes**.

> Je choisis le document sur lequel j'aurai le plus d'exemples concrets à donner spontanément.

DOCUMENT A

❝ *We like to give people the freedom to work where they want, safe in the knowledge that they have the drive and expertise to perform excellently, whether they (are) at their desk or in their kitchen.* ❞

Richard Branson, founder and chairman of Virgin

DOCUMENT B

Members of the Amalgamated Transit Union protest in support of Uber and Lyft drivers in New York on September 27th, 2016.

2 Expression orale en interaction ▶ 86, 87, 98

> Vous pouvez vous enregistrer et vous réécouter.

Vous disposez de **cinq minutes** pour vous entretenir avec l'examinateur au sujet de votre présentation et de questions plus générales.

Voici quelques questions que l'examinateur pourrait vous poser.

Does the fact that women go out to work help gender equality?

Private space and public space

Do you think people should be given the opportunity to work at home more?

What are the downsides of telecommuting (= *télétravail*)?

Would be be ready to share your car with strangers to make some money?

EXAM PREP

Évaluation 3 – Sujet 2 [20 points]

3ᵉ trimestre de Terminale
PARTIE 1 - Écrit

bordas
Flash PAGE
vidéo

bordas
Flash PAGE
PDF DYS

L'ensemble du sujet porte sur **l'axe 5** du programme : **Fictions et réalités**.

1 Compréhension de l'oral ▶ 46-53

▶ **Document 1** *Jenna Coleman on Playing Queen Victoria*
Source : **ITV, "Good Morning Britain", August 22ⁿᵈ, 2016**

En rendant compte, **en français**, du document, vous montrerez que vous avez identifié et compris :

VIDÉO
- sa nature et son thème principal ;
- les personnes qui s'expriment et leur témoignage ;
- la fonction et la portée du document (relater, informer, convaincre, critiquer, dénoncer, etc.).

2 Compréhension de l'écrit (3 861 signes) et de l'ensemble du dossier

▶ 54-67, 90

▶ **Document 2**

DYS

The story takes place around 1840 in a wealthy family's home with one daughter.

I do not doubt that they loved her – no one ever could who saw the way they looked at her. But they were people for whom love was a complicated affair, very closely bound up with, and easily confused with, matters of proprietorship, duty and control. Being who they were, the public eye upon them as it was, the honour of their family *so* great... well – there were *expectations*. They
5 wanted her well-mannered, modestly dressed, reserved and blushing, an immaculate prize for some wealthy noble with fine whiskers who could match or better the Vennaways' fortune and prestige.

They foresaw a future of stately grandeur for her – producing heirs, gracing society, decorating her husband's arm. Aurelia, however, had read too much and lived too little. Inspired by the vast
10 libraries of Hatville, and with no wise guide to understand or check her, every wild daydream seemed possible to her. She wanted a life of travel and intrigue, romances of her own choosing (she was determined there should be several) and to use her fortune and privilege to do philanthropic works. She wanted to be a new kind of role model for rich young ladies. ('Subversive and scandalous!' spat her father). She wanted her name in the history books, never mind that no
15 history book we had ever read recognised the opinions of women.

(...) She would come into her fortune in three short years, she argued; she had no need of a husband. She often pointed to the young queen as role model and exemplar. '*Victoria* refused to marry unless for love. Victoria seriously considered remaining unmarried, like Queen Elizabeth before her. Victoria only married her Albert because they have a *true understanding*.'

20 '*Her Majesty*,' roared her father, 'is queen of our nation and in a somewhat different position from you! Your responsibility, Aurelia, is not to govern the country and your duty is not to the people. It is to family. It is to marry and continue the Vennaway line. I have not been granted a son and I will *not* have my daughter fail me as well. *Her Majesty* is not my concern. You seem to think you have a choice in this Aurelia. I assure you that you do not.'

Tracy Rees, *Amy Snow,* 2015

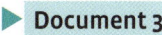

▶ Document 3

Queen Victoria is cool again. Who would have guessed?

Canada is the only country with an official holiday to mark Queen Victoria's birthday, which occurred 200 years ago this May 24. (…) But most Canadians, and most people, have been virtually ignoring the 19th-century's most influential female.
Until recently, that is.

5 Young women around the world are coming to view Victoria, who became queen at age 18, as a near-feminist icon, as someone they would like to be like.
It's a remarkable rediscovery of the monarch who oversaw the British Empire, which is associated with the things that contemporary culture condemns: colonialism, inequality and privilege. (…)
"I meet so many women who love Victoria. And I think the reason they love Victoria is she's the boss,"
10 says writer Daisy Goodwin, creator of the hit TV series *Victoria*, one of many recent dramas about the feisty queen, including films such as *The Young Victoria* and *Victoria and Abdul*.
"Young girls everywhere are really enjoying *Victoria*. I think that's because they identify with Victoria, because she's a young woman who isn't perfect, but is powerful," says Goodwin. "I have a 16-year-old daughter and I'm glad she's able to watch this show about a woman who calls the shots." (…)
15 While the Victorian era is often dismissed as rigid and stifling, it came with what even the skeptical American writer Mark Twain called "moral advancement." (…)
Women were given access to "a hundred bread-winning occupations," said Twain, including in medicine and the law. The modern newspaper became available to the common person.

Douglas Todd, vancouversun.com, May 17th, 2019

a. Compréhension du document 2.

Give an account of document 2 **in English** and in your own words, paying particular attention to:
  – the characters and how they are related;
  – the meaning of the sentence: 'there were *expectations*' (l. 4);
  – the main character's personality and her main influences;
  – the way women are considered in the society the characters belong to.

....
....
....
....
....
....
....
....
....
....
....
....
....
....
....
....
....
....
....

EXAM PREP

b. Compréhension du document 3.

Give an account of document 3 **in English** and in your own words, paying particular attention to:

– the main topic of the text;
– the event that prompted the writing of this article;
– the implications of the sentence: 'It is a remarkable rediscovery of the monarch' (line 7, paragraph 4);
– the way women's situation was changing at the time.

c. Compréhension de l'ensemble du dossier.

Consider the three documents (1, 2, 3) and explain briefly what makes Queen Victoria such a popular choice for works of fiction.

> Je liste les éléments explicites et implicites dans les trois documents qui peuvent servir à répondre à la question.

3 Expression écrite ▸ 68-71, 74, 78, 83, 96-99

Vous traiterez en anglais l'un des deux sujets suivants au choix. Répondez en 120 mots au moins.

● **Sujet A**

Write a speech for the renaming of your school after a famous person.

● **Sujet B**

Which opinion do you feel closest to? Why?

1 I believe historical dramas should be as close to reality as possible.

2 I don't mind if historical dramas are not historically accurate. It's the story I'm interested in.

3 Historical figures in a series are much easier to relate to than in a history book.

> Je m'inspire des films ou séries historiques que j'ai déjà vu(e)s pour trouver des idées.

....
....
....
....
....
....

Partie 2 - Oral 🗨️🗨️

4 Expression orale en continu ▶ 84, 87, 94-99

Choisissez parmi les documents A et B celui qui illustre le mieux, à votre sens, l'axe *Fictions et réalités*. Vous disposez de **10 minutes de préparation**. Puis **présentez et expliquez votre choix** en parlant pendant **cinq minutes**.

DOCUMENT A

Actress Jenna Coleman as Queen Victoria (1819-1901) in the British historical television drama series *Victoria*, aired in the UK on ITV in 2016. The Pilot episode tells the story of 18-year-old Princess Alexandrina Victoria, who becomes Queen after the death of her uncle King William IV.

> S'il me paraît difficile de parler d'un personnage historique, je peux choisir la citation qui me permet de donner des exemples plus personnels.

DOCUMENT B

> ❝ *Truth is stranger than fiction, but it is because fiction is obliged to stick to possibilities; truth isn't.* ❞
>
> **Mark Twain**, American writer of the 19th century

5 Expression orale en interaction ▶ 86, 87, 96-99

Vous disposez de **cinq minutes** pour vous entretenir avec l'examinateur au sujet de votre présentation et de questions plus générales.

Voici quelques questions que l'examinateur pourrait vous poser.

> Vous pouvez vous enregistrer et vous réécouter.

- Do you think historical dramas can help people discover history?

- If you could choose a series about any historical character, who would you choose and why?

Fictions and realities

- Do you personally watch historical TV series?

- Can we learn anything from fiction, even if we know it isn't true?

EXAM PREP

Évaluation 3 – Sujet 3 20 points

3ᵉ trimestre de Terminale
PARTIE 1 - Écrit

L'ensemble du sujet porte sur **l'axe 7** du programme : **Diversité et inclusion**.

1 Compréhension de l'oral ▶ 46-51

▶ **Document 1** *California Faces Crisis of Homelessness.*

Source : **NPR (National Public Radio), "Morning Edition", December 26ᵗʰ, 2019**

En rendant compte, **en français**, du document, vous montrerez que vous avez identifié et compris :

AUDIO

- sa nature et son thème principal ;
- les personnes qui s'expriment et leur témoignage ;
- la fonction et la portée du document (relater, informer, convaincre, critiquer, dénoncer, etc.).

> 💡 Je relève les références à des lieux pour situer le problème évoqué.

....
....
....
....
....
....
....
....
....
....

2 Compréhension de l'écrit (3 930 signes) et de l'ensemble du dossier

▶ 54-67, 90

▶ **Document 2**

It began to look as if I should be compelled to go to the very poor for my food. The very poor constitute the last sure recourse of the hungry tramp. The very poor can always be depended upon. They never turn away the hungry. Time and again, all over the United States, have I been refused food by the big house on the hill; and always have I received food from the little shack down by the creek or marsh, with its broken
5   windows stuffed with rags and its tired-faced mother broken with labor. Oh, you charity-mongers! Go to the poor and learn, for the poor alone are the charitable. They neither give nor withhold from their excess. They have no excess. They give, and they withhold never, from what they need for themselves, and very often from what they cruelly need for themselves. A bone to the dog is not charity. Charity is the bone shared with the dog when you are just as hungry as the dog.
10 There was one house in particular where I was turned down that evening. The porch windows opened on the dining room, and through them I saw a man eating pie – a big meat-pie. I stood in the open door, and while he talked with me, he went on eating. He was prosperous, and out of his prosperity had been bred resentment against his less fortunate brothers.
    He cut short my request for something to eat, snapping out, "I don't believe you want to work."
15 Now this was irrelevant. I hadn't said anything about work. The topic of conversation I had introduced was "food." In fact, I didn't want to work. I wanted to take the westbound overland that night.
    "You wouldn't work if you had a chance," he bullied.
    I glanced at his meek-faced wife, and knew that but for the presence of this Cerberus I'd have a whack at that meat-pie myself. But Cerberus sopped himself in the pie, and I saw that I must placate him if I were
20 to get a share of it. So I sighed to myself and accepted his work-morality.

Jack London, *The Road*, 1907

YS

▶ Document 3

Opinion: Being Hungry in America Is Hard Work. Food Banks Need Your Help

The first thing you learn when you rely on the food bank to feed your family is that you can't rely on the food bank to feed your family. Not entirely, anyway. The truth is, many families struggle with hunger despite regular visits to their local food pantry.

According to the most recent report from the US Department of Agriculture, 11.8 percent of Americans
5 are food insecure. I've experienced this first hand. I was a food bank customer myself – a single working mother whose paychecks barely covered rent, daycare, utilities and gas, let alone food.

My local food pantry was in the basement of a church. There was a wide parking lot to the side, but I always parked my car around the corner, where I'd be less likely to be spotted. I was already ashamed to be seen chugging along in a car with a smoking tailpipe and paying for fuel with stacks of change at
10 the gas station. I couldn't bear to have anyone know that I couldn't afford to feed my son.

The volunteers at the food bank were silver-haired and kind. On my first visit, I was fresh from my receptionist job, sharply dressed in a skirt suit handed down from my mother. I was worried I wouldn't look needy enough, so I'd tucked my pay stubs into my purse just in case. It wasn't necessary. I told the volunteers I needed help and they believed me. I didn't need to prove I was hungry. It was a time in
15 my life when I rarely received respect from anyone, but I received it from them. Dignity was the first gift they gave me.

A woman asked for my family size. I told her it was just me and my son and she wrote the information on an index card and tucked it away into a plastic box full of other cards. I thought about how each one of those index cards represented a person who had to walk through that door and ask for help like
20 I did. These were real people with lives, stories and families, shrunk so small they fit inside a box the size of a human hand. It was fitting. I felt small. Poverty had shrunk me.

Tamara Gane, npr.org, June 30ᵗʰ, 2019

a. Compréhension du document 2.

Give an account of document 2 **in English** and in your own words, paying particular attention to:
- the narrator and the situation;
- his feelings and opinion about poor people;
- the particular event he describes and the way he and the man feel about one another.

....
....
....
....
....
....
....
....
....
....
....
....
....
....

b. Compréhension du document 3.

Give an account of document 3 **in English** and in your own words, paying particular attention to:
- the narrator's past and present situation;
- her feelings about her situation;
- her feelings and opinion about the volunteers;
- the following quote: "I felt small. Poverty had shrunk me." (line 21, paragraph 5)

c. Compréhension de l'ensemble du dossier.

Consider the three documents (1, 2, 3) and explain briefly the impact poverty can have on people and the ways society reacts.

> Au brouillon, je fais un tableau à deux colonnes : dans la première, j'indique les effets de la pauvreté et l'état d'esprit des gens qui la subissent, dans la seconde les réactions positives et négatives de la société.

3 Expression écrite ▶ 68-71, 83, 89, 96-99

Vous traiterez en anglais l'<u>un des deux sujets suivants</u> au choix (120 mots au moins).

> Je prends le temps de réfléchir aux métaphores avant de commencer à rédiger.

- **Sujet A**

"A bone to the dog is not charity. Charity is the bone shared with the dog when you are just as hungry as the dog." (Text 1: line 8, paragraph 1). Give your opinion about the quote.

- **Sujet B**

You have been asked to write an article about food poverty. Begin with the sentence below:

According to the most recent report from the US Department of Agriculture, 11.8 percent of Americans are food insecure. (Text 2: line 4, paragraph 2)

....
....
....
....
....
....

PARTIE 2 - Oral

4 Expression orale en continu

▶ 84, 87, 96-99

Choisissez parmi les documents A et B celui qui illustre le mieux, à votre sens, l'axe *Diversité et inclusion*. Vous disposez de **10 minutes de préparation**. Puis **présentez et expliquez votre choix** en parlant pendant **cinq minutes**.

DOCUMENT A

Homelessness Reaches All-Time Record In New York City
A homeless man was photographed sleeping under an American Flag blanket on a park bench in 2013 in New York City. At that time there were 50,900 homeless people in New York City. Since then, homelessness has continued to grow. As of April 2021, over 53,199 people were homeless in New York City.

DOCUMENT B

According to a report written by the Council of Economic Advisers* in 2019, over half a million people go homeless every night in the United States. Approximately 65 percent are found in homeless shelters, and the other 35 percent sleep in places not intended for human habitation, such as sidewalks, parks, cars, or abandoned buildings. Homelessness almost always involves people facing desperate situations and extreme hardship.
* This is an agency within the Executive Office of the President, charged with offering the US President objective economic advice

5 Expression orale en interaction

▶ 86, 87, 96-99

Vous pouvez vous enregistrer et vous réécouter.

Vous disposez de **cinq minutes** pour vous entretenir avec l'examinateur au sujet de votre présentation et de questions plus générales.
Voici quelques questions que l'examinateur pourrait vous poser.

Is the American dream still possible in your opinion?

Can governments do more to promote social inclusion?

Diversity and inclusion

To what extent does being poor impact a child's chances of succeeding in an English-speaking country like the USA or the UK for example?

What do you think about the idea of a universal basic income?

EXAM PREP

Crédits photographiques

p. 6 © Christian Chavez/AP/SIPA • **p. 8** © UN Photo/Mark Garten/SIPA • **p. 10** © Discover Saint John • **p. 12** © vchal/iStock/GettyImages • **p. 14** © COLLECTION CHRISTOPHEL © Archives Stanley Kubrick / Metro Goldwyn Mayer • **p. 16** © Jim West/Alamy/Hemis • **p. 18** © Anthony Tusler • **p. 20** © Gregory Davies/Alamy/Hemis • **p. 22** © Shapiro, Mike/CartoonStock • **p. 23** © martin-dm/GettyImages • **p. 24** © Judd, Phil/CartoonStock • **p. 25** © Fuse/GettyImages • **p. 26** © MATTES René/hemis.fr • **p. 27** © Westend61/GettyImages • **p. 30** © Rank, Joseph/CartoonStock • **p. 31** © Drazen/GettyImages • **p. 31-Logo** © European Commission/DR • **p. 32** © Mark Anderson, www.andertoons.com • **p. 33** © Mark Peterson/REDUX-REA • **p. 35** © Peter Hatter/Age Fotostock • **p. 36** © Whitehead, Bill/ CartoonStock • **p. 40** © Manami Kimura/Shutterstock • **p. 41** © Mellish, Tim/CartoonStock • **p. 44** © Welleman, Peter/CartoonStock • **p. 45** © petekarici/iStock • **p. 49** © The Washington Post/Contributeur • **p. 53** © venimo/iStock • **p. 65** COLLECTION CHRISTOPHEL © Wilson Webb - Sony Pictures Entertainment - Columbia Pictures - New Regency Pictures - Pascal Pictures - Regency Enterprises • **p. 71** © PeopleImages/GettyImages • **p. 84-a** © MangoStar_Studio/GettyImages • **p. 84-b** © bymuratdeniz/GettyImages • **p. 84-c** © fizkes/GettyImages • **p. 84-d** © alvarez/GettyImages • **p. 84-e** © izusek/GettyImages • **p. 84-f** © Hola Images/GettyImages • **p. 85** © South Florida Business Journal • **p. 94** *Untitled* (Woman with daughter), 1990, silver print © Carrie Mae Weems. Courtesy of the artist and Jack Shainman Gallery, New York. • **p. 95** © MATTHEW ABBOTT/The New York Times-REDUX-REA • **p. 97** Edmund De Waal © Basso Cannarsa/Opale/Leemage • **p. 97** Flora Lewis © NYT/The New York Times-REDUX-REA • **p. 110** Dorothea Lange © The Granger Collection, New York/The Granger Collection/Coll. Christophel • **p. 114** © Nicholas MAC INNES/REA • **p. 119** © Drew Angerer/GETTY IMAGES NORTH AMERICA/AFP • **p. 123** © COLLECTION CHRISTOPHEL © ITV - Mammoth Screen • **p. 127 Document A :** © SPENCER PLATT / GETTY IMAGES NORTH AMERICA / Getty Images via AFP • **p. 127 Document B :** ©Fran/CartoonStock

Crédits textes

pp. 56-57-59-60 Excerpt(s) from *WAVE* by Sonali Deraniyagala, copyright © 2013 by Sonali Deraniyagala. Used by permission of Alfred A. Knopf, an imprint of the Knopf Doubleday Publishing Group, a division of Penguin Random House LLC. All rights reserved. • **p. 62** © Guardian News & Media Ltd 2020 • **pp. 65-67** © Guardian News & Media Ltd 2020 • **p. 76** earther.gizmodo.com. DR • **p. 89** p. © Guardian News & Media Ltd 2020 • **p. 91** Marcello Gleiser, DR • **p. 104** Richard Powers, *The Time of our Singing*, 2003. DR • **p. 105** Noah Berlatsky, nbcnews.com, January, 2nd 2019. DR • **p. 112** © Guardian News & Media Ltd 2020 • **p. 116** *Uberland* by Alex Rosenblat © 2018 by Alex Rosenblat. Published by the University of California Press • **p. 117** © Guardian News & Media Ltd 2020 • **p. 120** © 2015 Tracy Rees, reproduced by permission of Quercus Editions Limited • **p. 121** © Material republished with the express permission of: Vancouver Sun, a division of Postmedia Network Inc • **p. 125** © Tamara Gane

Crédits sonores

p. 48 WHYY, Inc. • **p. 50** © Voice of America • **p. 50** © Voice of America • **p. 51** © WYSO • **p. 51** © 2019 National Public Radio, Inc. Excerpt from news report titled "News For Teens, By A Teen" was originally broadcast on NPR's *Weekend Edition Sunday* on September 8, 2019, and is used with the permission of NPR. Any unauthorized duplication is strictly prohibited. • **p. 88** KJZZ. DR • **p. 100** © 2020 National Public Radio, Inc. Excerpt from news report titled "Santiago Potes Is 1st Latino DACA Recipient to Be Awarded Rhodes Scholarship" was originally broadcast on NPR's *Morning Edition* on December 8, 2020, and is used with the permission of NPR. Any unauthorized duplication is strictly prohibited. • **p. 101** © 2019 National Public Radio, Inc. Excerpt from news report titled "Managing Misinformation On Reddit" as originally broadcast on NPR's *Weekend Edition Sunday* on December 8, 2019, and is used with the permission of NPR. Any unauthorized duplication is strictly prohibited ; "People Working From Home Permanently Could Transform Rural America", NPR, Morning Edition, April 5th, 2021. DR. • **p. 102** © 2019 National Public Radio, Inc. Excerpt from news report titled "The Other Reasons Kids Aren't Getting Vaccinations: Poverty And Health Care Access" was originally broadcast on NPR's *All Things Considered* on May 20, 2019, and is used with the permission of NPR. Any unauthorized duplication is strictly prohibited ; © 2020 National Public Radio, Inc. Excerpt from news report titled "Lawrence Wright Wishes His Pandemic Novel Had Gotten It Wrong" was originally broadcast on NPR's *All Things Considered* on April 28, 2020, and is used with the permission of NPR. Any unauthorized duplication is strictly prohibited. • **p. 103** © 2021 National Public Radio, Inc. News report titled "A Racist Encounter Inspired 2 Teens To Publish A Magazine On The AAPI Experience" was originally broadcast on NPR's *Morning Edition* on May 21, 2021, and is used with the permission of NPR. Any unauthorized duplication is strictly prohibited. • **p. 116** © 2018 National Public Radio, Inc. Excerpt from news report titled "Ride-Hailing Services Add To Traffic Congestion, Study Says" was originally broadcast on NPR's *Morning Edition* on August 1, 2018, and is used with the permission of NPR. Any unauthorized duplication is strictly prohibited. • **p. 124** © 2019 National Public Radio, Inc. Excerpt from news report titled "California Faces Crisis Of Homelessness" was originally broadcast on NPR's Morning Edition on December 26, 2019, and is used with the permission of NPR. Any unauthorized duplication is strictly prohibited.

Nous avons cherché en vain les éditeurs et les ayants droit de certains textes et photos reproduits dans ce manuel ainsi que certains audios. Leurs droits sont réservés aux Éditions Bordas (DR).

Responsable éditoriale : Céline Ullas assistée de Zoé Dakszewicz
Directrice éditoriale : Véronique Gilles de la Londe
Directeur artistique : Pierre Taillemite
Droits étrangers et préparation copie : Aurore Kauffmann
Iconographie : Émilie Réaux
Conception et réalisation de la maquette : Joëlle Parreau
Conception et illustration de couverture : Jérémie Clayes
Relecture : Gilles Chauvin
Fabrication : Françoise Leroy
Gravure : Irilys
Réalisation sonore : Quali'sons

MIXTE
Papier issu de sources responsables
FSC www.fsc.org FSC® C022030

Bordas est un éditeur qui s'engage pour la préservation de l'environnement et utilise du papier issu de forêts gérées de manière responsable et d'autres sources contrôlées.

Ce cahier a été imprimé en France en juillet 2021 par Imprimerie de Champagne, imprimeur certifié IMPRIM'VERT

N° de projet : 10275451
Dépôt légal : avril 2020